FIVE TO EIGHT

Dorothy Butler first became interested in the subject of children and their reading while teaching English in a secondary school. Her interest was focused on the pre-school years when her own children (she has two sons and six daughters) were small, and she became involved with the work of the Play Centre Association in New Zealand. As her children grew up, she started her own business from home, selling children's books and providing an advisory service for parents.

Dorothy Butler continues to run her highly successful bookshop in Auckland, lectures and writes about children's books, runs a Reading Centre for children who need help, and still manages to enjoy time spent with her thirteen grandchildren and the rest of her large family.

In 1980 Dorothy Butler received the prestigious Eleanor Farjeon Award in recognition of her outstanding services to children and books.

D0994732

DOROTHY·BUTLER

Five to Eight

with drawings by Shirley Hughes

THE BODLEY HEAD

LONDON

ALSO BY DOROTHY BUTLER

Babies Need Books
Cushla and Her Books

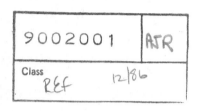

9002001 ATR

Class REF 12/86

British Library Cataloguing in
Publication Data
Butler, Dorothy
Five to eight.
1. Reading (Primary)
I. Title
372.4   LB1525
ISBN 0–370–30672–4

© Dorothy Butler 1986
Illustrations © Shirley Hughes 1986
Printed in Finland for
The Bodley Head Ltd,
30 Bedford Square, London WC1B 3RP
by Werner Söderström Oy
Phototypeset in Baskerville
by Wyvern Typesetting Limited, Bristol
First published 1986

For Catherine
Christine
Patricia
Vivien
Anthony
Simon
Susan
and Josephine
who taught me about children
in the beginning

ACKNOWLEDGEMENTS

My formal thanks are due to Methuen Children's Books Ltd, UK, E. P. Dutton, USA, and the Canadian Publishers, McClelland and Stewart Ltd for permission to use lines from 'Pooh Goes Visiting' from *Winnie-the-Pooh* by A. A. Milne as display lettering in the prelims and also to Oxford University Press for permission to use lines from 'The Connemara Donkey' from *The Little Book Room* by Eleanor Farjeon as display lettering to precede Chapter 1.

My thanks are also due to the publishers who have supplied information about books mentioned in the text. My publishers have done their best to ensure that all details and attributions are correct; however, any errors will naturally be rectified in any future reprint.

D. B.

CONTENTS

'How long does getting thin take?' asked Pooh anxiously.

'About a week, I should think.'

'But I can't stay here for a *week*!'

'You can *stay* here all right, silly old Bear. It's getting you out which is so difficult.'

'We'll read to you,' said Rabbit cheerfully.

A. A. Milne, from 'Pooh Goes Visiting',
in *Winnie-the-Pooh*

To Begin With . . .

This is the second manual I have written for parents. The first was called *Babies Need Books* and was aimed at persuading parents to use books with their children from the earliest months of life. It covered the years from birth to about six: the most important years of all, if children are to be launched into the world as confident, intelligent, contributing people. I believe this even more deeply as time passes and evidence accumulates. But I realize that 'the next stage up' has special needs and puzzling aspects, too. In particular, it takes in the potentially hazardous 'learning to read' stage.

'What books do you recommend for Jenny, who is five?' asked a father who wrote to me some time ago. 'Infant "readers" seem so dull after the stories we've been reading to her at home.' This request cheered me, while it set me thinking about writing this book. Jenny's father clearly wanted reading to be fun for his daughter. He feared that the stilted, passionless stuff of which so many graded 'schemes' are made might adversely affect her attitude to reading.

His concern, while justified, was probably unnecessary; such a child's experience of good books, read aloud at home, usually bears her safely through the most boring scheme. But not always.

It does seem that even well-prepared children—those who encounter books early and have parents who talk to them, listen to them and read aloud to them—sometimes have difficulties when 'school' reading begins. There is, certainly, an increased tendency these days for parents to feel apprehensive about this stage. In many cases, this very anxiety produces tension in the child, and serves to create problems which, against a more relaxed background, might not have arisen.

I believe that prevention is always better than cure, and that positive, constructive measures used by ordinary people who care are likely in the end to be more effective than the skilled and scientific procedures of specialists. Most of all, I believe in the power of parents in children's lives.

Children are learning to read from the time they are born. The sights and sounds of their world fuel the fires of their developing minds from earliest days, providing a basis for all future learning. But the sights and the sounds of the modern world can be confusing, rather than helpful.

Children need contact and response; ever-present opportunities to forge relationships, to communicate. And who are better placed than parents to provide these opportunities?

Listening to stories—to one's own native tongue used in narrative and description—is the first and fundamental step on the road to independent reading.

The child who is listening expertly is using the senses and techniques which the mature reader uses. She is able to absorb and process a stream of language, arranging ideas so that the author's message is understood and building, step-by-step, a mental picture of the whole.

Expectation of meaning is vital to the reading task, and occurs automatically in the child who is accustomed to listening. De-coding the symbol is the simplest part of reading. Responding to the complex message of a page of print is the test; a test which the well-read-to child passes with flying colours.

Children with well-nourished minds draw on a deep well of concept and vocabulary to sustain their performance in the reading task. Response, that vital component, is automatic if conversation and stories have been part of daily life from the beginning.

That this nourishment must continue, without interruption, through schooldays, should hardly need stating. Side by side with early reading-alone on the child's part should go reading-aloud on the part of the adult. How else can children learn that reading is uniquely enjoyable, that books are wells of wonder and information? Years may pass before the child's skill in reading catches up with his other interests and understanding. A seven-year-old child, satisfactorily acquiring reading skills, may be able to read the excellent stories in the World's Work I Can Read series, the spirited Bodley Beginners and the entertaining Happy Families tales, published by Viking Kestrel. The same child will listen with absorption and delight to Clive King's *Stig of the Dump* and to E. B. White's *Charlotte's Web*, both of which books require nine- or ten-year-old reading skills, but speak directly to the increasingly reflective seven-year-old. How is the six-year-old mind to be nourished, the seven-year-old intelligence to be extended, if we withhold the simply supplied benefits of reading-aloud?

The main purpose of this second book is to persuade parents to continue reading aloud to their children during their school years—or to begin, if the practice has not been established earlier. Because I believe that 'nothing succeeds like success', I have supplied titles and descriptions of several hundred books which I know to have been successful with children of the age I am considering: from five to eight. Naturally, not all books will have a similar impact on all children, but I have included only titles which I have read myself and believe to be good books.

I have used the first chapter to describe the sort of background against which I believe most children might become readers. More specifically, I have suggested ways in which those adults who are in control of children's lives might alter or modify conditions which keep children and books apart. I believe that these conditions abound in the modern world.

In Chapter 6 I have described, as clearly as possible, the reading process. Naturally, this is a personal view. I have tried to sketch the existing state of knowledge about reading in terms which the non-specialist person will understand. I believe that most parents are under-informed in this area, and that much might be accomplished by increased understanding.

You may wish to read this chapter, entitled 'Learning to Read', before you begin the rest of the book, or as it comes. It is included merely as background to the more important concern: that of helping you to identify books for your five-to-eight-year-olds that will enthuse them, and help you to avoid the apprehension which sometimes assails parents, and is invariably passed on to children.

Although it is desirable that parents and teachers should keep in touch, it is useless to pretend that parents will always get the understanding and help they need. Teachers range from the superb to the abysmal, from the likeable to the disagreeable—as do all other sections of the community, including parents! Avoiding confrontation is a safe policy if you sense any serious difference of values or opinion. If you are confident that you *are* providing the things your child needs to become a good reader, you can usually avoid tension between home and school. Chapter 6 will help, I hope.

I believe that learning to read is too important to be left to chance, or to schools, and that parents, whose influence in children's lives eclipses that of all officials and institutions, should take positive action to ensure that their children become fluent, joyful and voluntary readers. I *know* that parents can do this, given confidence in their own capacity, a few fundamental facts about the reading task, a belief in books and a little help in finding suitable titles.

Accordingly, Chapters 2, 3, 4 and 5 consist of information about particular books. I have, again, adopted an 'age-group' division, with a great deal of overlap. Borderlines are blurred at this stage; many books which eight-year-olds can read to themselves will be enjoyed by younger children, if obliging adults will read them aloud. And some six-year-olds, of course, read as fluently as eight-year-olds, or even older children.

It seems that only a particular sort of person can write convincingly for the five-to-eights; perhaps a person who has an acute memory for the way it *feels* to be beyond babyhood but still not a truly independent child. Adult memory is usually strongest for a later period of childhood. Our recalled activities and passions at ten and twelve have, for most of us, an intensity which does not characterize our memories of five and seven. Even though what happens to us in our earliest years may have lasting effects on our minds and emotions, its impact is likely to be unconscious. Few of us can remember how it *felt*.

Most of the so-called 'classics' have been written for children of, roughly, ten to fourteen. The reasons for this are easy to understand, if one considers a few simple facts. To begin with, it is reasonable to expect that children over eight will be able to read fluently. This assumption means that authors need not confine themselves to simple vocabulary and sentence structure. (It is commonly considered to be difficult, if not impossible, to write simply and still produce work of high literary quality, though an occasional rare book gives the lie to this belief.)

It is true, however, that authors must limit themselves to relevant themes for this younger age-group and this may demand a degree of irksome restraint. Children between five and eight are still dependent on adults; one cannot imagine them coping alone on desert islands, banished to distant planets, or cut off from help by fire or flood. Of course, they may be part of family groups which contend with these, and other hazards, but their roles will be minor ones. In fact, their very dependence may be used by authors to illustrate the sterling qualities of older sisters or brothers, as in Walter Macken's splendid story, *The Flight of the Doves*. ·

Some publishers have made spirited attempts to cater for the five-to-eights, and their efforts must be recognized and applauded. Both picture books and older novels are, as categories, eligible for yearly prizes which bring prestige to author and publisher alike. By contrast, simple novels for beginning readers attract cursory, if any, attention at all, and almost never feature in prize lists. Books for the five-to-eights—hard to write, hard to review, hard to market—seem to occupy a sort of literary no-man's-land.

One must forgive the parents of this age-group for their uncertainty—even confusion—on the subject of book provision. It is shared by many professionals! How does one assess an 'early reader'—or a large print novel for a seven-year-old? What points should one look for? What do children of this age want in their books, expect in their books, *need* in their books? Is there any way of judging books, short of reading them aloud and gauging their effect on listeners of appropriate age? And does the 'early reading' book have any place outside the schoolroom? It is all very puzzling.

I believe, however, that there *is* a satisfactory starting-place for parents. Books, throughout life, nourish the whole person. Identifying the characteristics of children of five, six, seven and eight, even in a general way, must cast some light on their needs. Recognizing the books which will help to meet these needs then starts to be possible. We may not know *exactly* what we are looking for, but we have narrowed the field. Within this field, a developing awareness of child response—an awareness which increases with trial, error and experience—will be an invaluable asset.

As before, I have discussed the children themselves at some length. What to expect of children at various ages is a common area of concern among parents, the cause of much doubt on the one side and distress on the other.

Inevitably, my own family creeps in at points. At the time of writing, six of my thirteen grandchildren fall in age between almost five and eight-and-a-half. All of these children live close to me and are part of my life. They are all very different from one another, but have one thing in common: they all love listening to stories. Was ever a child born who *didn't*, if the story was worth the telling?

I like to think that the exclusive nature of my experience with my grandchildren is offset by my work with a wider range of children in my day-to-day work. Six years ago, I set up in Auckland a Reading Centre, which offers help to children whose reading accomplishment has been unsatisfactory in some way. The methods used in this Centre are based on my belief in story, and on the relationship of listening to learning to read. Crucial to the process is the provision of the right books: books which will make a child's eye sparkle, a child's hand want to grab.

Some of our Reading Centre children have real disabilities, some are suffering from the crippling effects of apparent failure and, for a few, English is a second language. Inevitably, some of my 'Centre' children will find their way into this book, even if mention of them is not specific. They, also, are very much part of my life.

You may be asking by now: Is this a book about reading aloud to children, or about helping children to learn to read? To which I reply, 'Both. They are two sides of the one coin.'

I

Raising Readers

'What a lot of nonsense you tell the child,' she smiled. 'You stuff him as full of tales as you stuff your pipe with baccy.'

'What else would ye stuff a pipe with, or a child?' asked Mr O'Toole.

Eleanor Farjeon, from 'The Connemara Donkey',
included in *The Little Bookroom*

If reading is to benefit a child, it must become part of that child's life. Not as a task to be mastered, not as a mark or a grade on a school report, but as a living activity, as normal and essential as eating or sleeping.

Real readers read for the sake of reading, not to collect facts, nor to pass examinations, nor merely to fill in time on trains and aeroplanes (though they certainly do these things, too). Real readers read because they have come to know and to need that special nourishment of mind and spirit which comes from books, and so cannot live without them. For reading is not merely a school subject. It is a tool for living, a tool which will be refined and polished to the end of life by those who come to know its worth.

Unfortunately, the only people who really understand this truth are the real readers. These are the people whose houses are inevitably full of books, both owned and borrowed. Not surprisingly, most of their children catch the condition early in life. It is wrong, however, to imagine that any particular virtue attaches to this state; it is mainly a thing of luck or circumstance. But the phenomenon is worth looking at by those who, for one reason or another, want their children to become committed readers and were not themselves snared by books early in life. What are the features of these 'reading' homes which seem to produce readers?

To begin with, there is adult example, during the years when example *works*. It is typical of children under about nine that they admire their parents, and want to be like them. As one cannot count on this ambition to endure much beyond this point, it is vital to turn it to good use while it lasts. But you cannot deceive children. Acclaiming a lifestyle which you do not practise yourself does not work, at any age. If you do not read for enjoyment, as part of your daily life, it is useless to commend the practice to your children.

So you must make an effort. If you don't belong to a library already, join one, and make sure that your child sees you poring over a book at least once every day. This need not be a novel; it may be a book on gardening or cooking, fishing or building a bookcase. Such books usually have illustrations, which you can share with other family members, especially the children. You will be amazed and delighted at the range of books available, once you start. Try to make this library visit a weekly outing for the whole family, adult and child. Joint examination of books on return home will be savoured—with the television set mercifully mute in the corner, once the books take over.

Next, consider the possibility of adding fiction to your own reading diet. Even here, it is possible to find something which you and your children can enjoy together. Everyone loves James Herriot's books about his veterinary ventures in the depths of Yorkshire, for example. Chunks of these hilarious and wholesome tales can be read aloud to the whole family—after a meal, perhaps, or any time when you are all together. 'Hey, you lot, listen to this!' is an irresistible injunction.

Then, explore the paperback section in your local bookshop. The example of keen book *ownership* is of the utmost importance if you hope to raise readers. Make it clear to the children that *your* needs as well as theirs must be considered in the allocation of family income. *You* want to buy a book this week, and resources won't stretch to two. Your children's estimation of the value of the book will rise steeply at this evidence of adult enthusiasm, even if they protest at your selfishness!

It is obvious that there must be *time* in a child's life, if a love of books is to take root and grow. Obvious, but constantly overlooked. Time is, in fact, deplorably unavailable in the lives of modern children, and is likely to be especially absent from the daily round of the so-called 'privileged' child. Many such children are over-organized and over-transported; they belong to too many clubs and have too many lessons. Many of them spend a considerable portion of their waking hours being collected and delivered, like parcels. Before long, remedial reading must be fitted in somehow between piano lessons and gymnastics, scouts and swimming. Small wonder that most of them slump in front of the television set when they finally arrive home.

What has happened to their childhood—that time of exuberance, wonder and sudden whim, of yearning ache and spontaneous laughter, of inexpressible lassitude and wild, impromptu action? Do our children ever lie and look at the sky any longer?

Time to read . . . and a place to read *in*. The modern small living-room or lounge has, more likely than not, a television set in prime position. In many homes, almost all family activities are conducted within sight and sound of the 'box'; meals are eaten, family discussions conducted, children received from school and finally despatched to bed—all to the accompaniment of strident sound and flashing image. Many of today's children have never known what it is to be alone, in the true sense; alone to think, to experiment with whatever comes to hand, to 'muck about', to doodle, to savour past experience and anticipate future.

Modern houses need, desperately, some substitute for those prized retreats familiar to earlier generations: curtain-shrouded window seats, attics, porches, spare rooms, wood-sheds, wash-houses . . . Even the good old privy, decently screened with vine-hung trellis, was a place of sanctuary in the past. (You could pretend not to hear, when hailed from the house.)

Sadly, although the need has increased in modern times, the practice of retreat itself has become all but impossible for many children. We cannot return to an earlier lifestyle; we are committed to what we have. But we can recognize our children's need for quiet space, and use our ingenuity and imagination to help. Even if a child must share a bedroom (and we all did *that* in the old days), surely we can arrange a 'very own' corner for each child. Individual bookcases, constructed simply from planks and bricks, can be placed close to beds. A personal reading lamp for a child may be the deciding factor in establishing the time-honoured habit of reading in bed. (Surely the most luxurious of all human self-indulgences!) An extra pillow—or better still, a few large, comfortable cushions so that the bed can be used as a place of retreat during the day—and you will have carved for each child a personal refuge from the world.

As soon as possible (perhaps between five and six) start encouraging children to monitor their own sleeping times. Fix a bedtime, but not a 'lights-out', as long as the time is used for reading, or looking at books. The youngest children usually fall asleep quite soon, and the older ones can be left safely to read. They will otherwise employ the old torch-under-the-bedclothes routine as their addiction grows, anyway. Most people grow up believing themselves to need more sleep than they actually do. Let's not perpetuate the delusion in our children. It is boredom that leads to fatigue. These kids are not going to be bored!

What about a bedtime story? By all means, if you can manage it, but you need not feel guilty, if you can't. The criterion is the *frequency* with which you read to your children, not the time or place. Different families will have different ideas and habits, according to size and living pattern. Our own family was a large one, and we fell into the habit of regular evening reading in the living-room. During the day, anywhere and anytime was considered suitable for a story, depending only on adult capitulation to frequent plea.

During weekends and holidays, our large double bed was popular for reading sessions. This was a splendid roosting place, especially on wet days. Memories of the snug, shared pleasure of Rumer Godden's Dolls' House books, read one after the other during a winter holiday fortnight when the rain poured down, return at the mere mention, with the smell and sound of messy toffee-making sessions in the kitchen, and the necessity of clambering over intricate clothes-horse, chair and blanket constructions in the living-room.

You must face the fact early that a reading household is seldom a very tidy one. But books and children grace a home, and the children will not be there for long. Tell yourself, as often as necessary, that 'people are more important than things'. Try, during the precious years of your children's childhood, to accept them as they are: by nature grubby, irreverent, insubordinate, quarrelsome, always hungry, forever wanting to touch, to open, to push, never wanting to wait. . .

If you apply yourself to the business of getting to know your daughters and sons, you will discover that their vices are actually their virtues in disguise. Children are close to the earth, honest, outspoken in the cause of justice and quick to recognize insincerity. They are determined to learn the facts and skills *they* know they need to face the world (as against those *we* believe they need), they have acute, if untamed, senses of humour, infinite willingness to forgive *us* our failings, boundless curiosity and bottomless wells of energy, of every sort. Their good cheer and the stoutness of their hearts passes all understanding, given the state of the world they find themselves committed to. Their tragedy is that the torrent of their wonderful capacities may be reduced to a trickle by the time they have 'grown up'.

'Why is the world full of brilliant children and dud grown-ups?' asked G. K. Chesterton. Why, indeed.

It is no use expecting children of five to eight to maintain a high degree of order and neatness in their lives, for they do not value such things. If you *insist* on order, you may even be investing in trouble later. Many an adolescent, who is kicking over the traces in dangerous areas of life, is merely rebelling against an unreasonably strict code imposed earlier. Cause and effect are still a little cloudy, for the five-to-eights. Books may be walked on, sat on, crammed into school bags next to dripping-wet swimming-suits or decomposing banana skins, and amazed grief, mixed with indignation, meet the resultant damage.

It is wise to keep cautions to a minimum. Example is always the best teacher. Such practices as turning the page at the corner, using a bookmark instead of leaving the book open face downwards and using a plastic bag for carrying can become part of normal book-handling. But don't expect early independence in this field, any more than in other areas of behaviour. Help and example bear fruit in the end and make for friendly relations meanwhile. 'Let's put the books away together,' is always preferable to a curt 'Tidy up the books now.' Commands are resented, where cheerful pleas for help are usually met. Children can be tired, bad-tempered, or upset, just as their elders can—and haven't had years of practice in coping with their feelings. Avoiding issues with this age-group pays off. You can win only by using your greater strength, and this is not an advantage which is going to last.

Most dangerous of all is the risk of turning children away from reading by your insistence on impossibly high standards of book handling. It is understandable that adults should be conscious of the *cost* of any article which they have bought. But the only way to get one's money's worth out of a book is to make sure it is *read*, and in the case of children's books, this means wear and tear. A well-loved book is bound to be scruffy in the end; scruffy and read. Worth what one paid for it in the first place.

Years ago, we bought an inexpensive set of encyclopedias

for our children. These became a staple source of information. 'Who's got K to L?' was a constant cry—and one of our very small children learned her alphabet by arranging all twelve volumes on the shelf in correct order, every night for weeks.

A neighbouring family was inveigled by a door-to-door salesman into buying a much more costly set of encyclopedias for their children. They paid, in monthly instalments over a year, about ten times the price of our set. Sadly, their children had little benefit from their beautifully bound books. So many hand-washing, table-clearing stipulations surrounded their use that it was easier to give up. 'They're too hard, anyway,' I heard one of their children tell one of ours, who was anxious to get his (no doubt grubby) hands on them. He didn't succeed, despite persistence.

If you are already a committed reader yourself, you may be prey to pangs of guilt about your tendency to disappear into a novel when the rest of the world is mowing its lawns and cleaning its windows. You may relax. My children have assured me that my tendency to disappear into a book was a godsend to them during childhood. Other mothers they could name noticed *everything* their children did that was not allowed, whereas I could be relied upon for a certain quality of abstractedness. (I am bound to admit, even now, to a tendency to slip off into contemplation of another world— the one in which the characters in my latest novel are coping, or not coping, with their lives.)

A great fortifier, the book. And a bulwark too. I remember returning from an evening class which I used to teach, to hear my husband's voice droning on in a bedroom shared by two of our children, when the hour indicated that these two would probably be asleep. They were. My questioning gaze elicited from my husband the explanation that he had wanted to find out what happened.

'Couldn't you have read it to yourself, in more comfort?' I enquired.

'No,' he said. 'I've a mountain of papers to mark.' (He taught evening classes, too.)

I do not propose to tell you how to cope with the inroads of television on your family life, because I find the subject depressing, and I want this to be a cheerful book. I can only suggest that 'as little as possible' is the best maxim, if you want to raise readers. I must add the caution that parents, also, (or perhaps especially) must embrace the policy, if it is to work for their children. Experience of interaction—real person in communication with real person—is what we all need, and the number of hours in each day is limited.

Many recent books have examined the effect of extensive television viewing on children's lives; it is not my intention to quote their findings, or their warnings. Instead, I want to persuade you that time spent with your children, exchanging ideas, narrating experiences, laughing at the ridiculous and wondering at the wonderful, with books supporting and surprising, will help to give you all a good and satisfying life. I hope I can do this, or at least persuade you to try the formula.

2

Five-Year-Olds and Their Books

Five-year-olds are enjoyable people. Their belief in adults as fountains of love, wisdom and support is flattering, and their needs are easy to meet. They like to be acceptable, in the main, and this means a reduction of that risk-anything insubordination which seemed to characterize their behaviour in the preceding year. Of course, five-year-olds are also as different, one from the other, as are fifteen-year-olds or forty-five-year-olds. But, like the members of these other age-groups, they have much in common.

Five-year-olds are at the crossroads. At home, particularly if there are one or more younger children, they seem large, competent and bossy. Their joy in their own apparent strength bubbles over into wild action; they play indefatigably, indoors and out, devising games which reflect their entire repertoire of experience, both first- and secondhand: from shopkeeper through doctors and nurses to Superman, all in a single afternoon. Sometimes, they seem drunk with the sheer joy of being alive.

Wise parents of five-year-olds postpone plans for home redecoration which include fragile, handmade ornaments and pastel furnishings, unless their home is large enough to provide an 'out-of-bounds to children' section. (Shades of the Victorian parlour!)

This is seldom possible in the average modern house, and has its limitations as a policy, anyway. Furniture can be stout and functional and still attractive, and prohibitions few but sensible. Of course, there must be limits; but if their infringement (inevitable, occasionally) leads to real damage or disaster, there will always be tension in the family.

Children must have scope for imaginative games, if their minds, bodies and spirits are to be nourished. By this provision for creative play during childhood, we encourage their development into competent and responsible adults.

School as a hurdle must not be underestimated in the life of the five-year-old. Pre-school groups are for fun; school is in deadly earnest. We may make light of it, but the message is received. For better or worse, school-starters enter a huge, bureaucratic organization which will seem to possess them for an unimaginable period of time. (Remember that five-year-olds find it impossible to imagine next week.) Requirements are made of them, inexorably, whether they value or understand these demands or not—or want to be thrust out from the comfortable security of their homes, into this strange, new, dazing environment, anyway. Some of the most original children are the least conforming. Other children naturally prefer a degree of order and peace. To these children, the jungle of the large school playground must seem like a nightmare, full of roaring noise and violent action.

In this setting, the 'big' five-year-old is very small indeed, and may feel even smaller. For five-year-old competence is only skin deep. Obliged for the first time in their lives to keep track of personal possessions, five-year-olds need constant servicing from adults. 'Where is your jersey (shoes, school lunch, handkerchief, book, bus fare, raincoat)?' and other reasonable demands, bounce endlessly off the bemused school-starter. Understanding of cause and effect is minimal at this stage, and likely to be reduced by the sheer trauma of new demands and circumstances.

But appearances must be kept up in public, and this means that home and family must take up the slack. The phenomenon of the well-behaved school-attender (aged five) who collapses into an ungovernable passion on arrival home is well known to experienced parents. Language in the service of reason avails us little, here. We must treat this exhausted, over-stimulated, confused and despairing human being as a two-year-old, gather her up and find some way of establishing home base as a warm and accepting haven all over again.

Don't imagine that this is easy, or that what works for one child will necessarily work for another. The art is to help the child to learn to cope with her own reaction to stress; a lifetime problem for all of us, actually. We expect a lot of these small, inexperienced people.

Some parents resort to television as a pacifier at this stage. Certainly, its capacity to remove human attention from the real scene of action, without itself making any intellectual demands, is impressive. But do we want to produce a human being who switches on the television set when the going gets tough? What about helping children to accept their own and other people's reaction to life as it is, the opportunity to start developing strategies for coping with reality? This is what we all need, and I don't believe that it is advanced by the use of the flickering screen as a mindless comfort.

The habit of an after-school story session, once the pattern is set, will become a strength; something for both the child and the parent to look forward to. This is an age when all children love individual parental attention.

Certainly, differences in temperament play their part in establishing needs. For some people, life will always be more difficult than for others. But for most, the sixth year of life has particular trials. Allowances must be made.

And the passage of time does help. Five-year-olds *want* to be acceptable, and are now prey to painful embarrassment when things get out of hand. Their growing understanding of the way things *should* be done is in strong contrast to their capacity for accomplishment.

They still need shelter from possible failure and unwelcome limelight, and look to us, their family, for this protection. Our support must be total. We expect a lot from our children; temporary adjustment of our own lifestyle is more than justified in their cause.

Nor should we be lulled into a belief that problems solved

will *stay* solved, in the early years. Almost all children, at some stage during their first year at school, are swamped, suddenly, by the realization that their lives have been taken over by 'the system'; that their range of choices has narrowed drastically, if not dried up utterly. Resentment, if not open revolt, may result—and is as common in the confident as in the apprehensive child. (The cheerful, outgoing youngster *expects* to have some say in his own destiny, and may be outraged to discover that this is a vain hope!)

Extra support is needed in the face of such reaction. More attention at home, small after-school treats and an occasional day off will help. Evidence is required that people really do care, and are prepared to support. Accompanying, rather than despatching the child to school for a time may help, and avoiding recriminations certainly will. It is easy to slip into panicky verbal reaction—we are all thrown off our perches when our apparently stable offspring show signs of rebellion. 'Don't be silly—you're a big girl now, and you *like* school!''Look at Peter!' (who started last week, and is bathed in new-found glory). 'He's much younger than you and *he* isn't making a fuss!'

The whole of life—our own, as well as our children's—is a complicated and messy business, at best. We never progress in any field, but that we slip back a few notches in another. Some days we know we are operating below par. We suspect that we would be better tomorrow, if we were able to walk on the hills today . . . but we have been brought up to believe that work, however unrewarding, is good for us, and we press on.

We must, at all costs, avoid conditioning our children for a world which is ceasing to exist. We cannot know what lies ahead for them, but we can be sure of one thing. Qualities of originality, flexibility and good humour have always helped human beings to lead good lives, even in difficult times, and we must try to believe that they always will. Any other course has us defeated at the outset. We must, and *can* fortify and equip our children by our love and concern for them, and by the example we give them of our own energetic involvement in the affairs of our immediate world.

And books will help us to do this, immeasurably.

Five-year-olds are ready for a wide range of books. While continuing to love picture books (as indeed they will, throughout this whole period and beyond), they will listen, increasingly, to stories without pictures, or with very few.

Learning to listen—'to make the pictures in your own head', as one of my children described the process—must be seen as an important skill for the five-year-old. Evidence exists that, in our over-graphic world, many children lag in this capacity, with serious results at a later stage. Recent research reveals that students of seventeen and eighteen years of age commonly have listening difficulties which have nothing to do with deafness; they merely cannot construct mental concepts from heard, or read, language, without the help of pictures or diagrams. This is, of course, a serious handicap, for the ear surpasses all other organs as an implement of effective learning.

If you find this hard to believe, think of the plight of totally deaf children. Because they find it so hard to learn to speak and to read, the majority of deaf children have limited chances of reaching their full intellectual potential. By contrast, blind children, their ears alert to the language around them and with braille books at their disposal, may keep pace with their normally equipped contemporaries, and even, helped by the development of compensatory senses, outstrip them intellectually.

Blindness is a tragic disability; but it does not compare with deafness in its capacity to limit or distort the growth of mind and personality. When one considers that the students described above were *not* deaf, but merely incapable of using their physically perfect senses of hearing, through the influences of the environment which the modern world provides for them, there is certainly cause for alarm.

There can be no doubt that the capacity to listen—

responsively and imaginatively—is one which we must help children to develop. Just as certainly, recourse to books, as sources of material which will induce this sort of listening, is not only sensible, but imperative.

Ideally, the five-year-old child has been listening to stories without pictures for at least a year. If this has not been the case, then I would suggest a special effort, perhaps in the proportion of one story without illustrations, to two picture books. If the child seems reluctant to make the change, I would give practice in listening to a *told* story, rather than a tale from a book. You need not feel unequipped for this task. Every time we say to a friend, 'Guess what happened yesterday!', we are launching into a storytelling venture—and most of us do it well!

Some people are born storytellers. Usually, the art comes so easily that they neither recognize nor value it. They just love telling anyone who will listen about things which have happened to themselves, or to other people. Their reward comes in the response of their listeners: rapt and goggle-eyed attention, as like as not.

Family life provides a rich source of such tales, which, like the best traditional stories, grow in the telling. (The time our year-old baby was seen to be wearing her upturned bowl of porridge as a hat . . . the famous day on which our four-year-old, shrouded to his ankles in a cardboard box, walked over the edge of the terrace and bowled down the hill . . . No one, least of all the central figure in the drama, has ever tired of hearing about these and other homely catastrophes. All families have them, surely! Your material is there and waiting.)

The next step is, of course, to produce a book without pictures; and it helps to explain the process to the young listener, in simple terms. The following example fell into my lap a week ago. My son-in-law, David, was reading to my grandson, Oliver, on the beach. They were both lying on the sand, and David was holding the book (*The Adventures of Sam Pig* by Alison Uttley) at arm's length, using it as a shield from the sun. 'Bring it closer! I can't *see!*' said Oliver, with the bossiness of the five-year-old to his nearest and dearest. David pointed out that, since there was not a picture in sight, Oliver might as well lie back, close his eyes and make the pictures in his head. Oliver complied with this suggestion, and after a short while said, 'I'm doing it, Dad! It works!'

Oliver has always gazed intently at a book, whether or not it has pictures. His cousin Christopher, by contrast, gazes into the distance, his eyes reflecting in turn the changing mood and pace of the story. Cousin Hannah does both, dreamily gazing at nothing in particular, but returning to a book at intervals to ask, 'Where are we up to?' A finger pointing to the relevant line satisfies her.

What is going on in each very different child's mind? Do they reflect on the process by which the reading adult converts print into sensible language, or do they believe that some sort of magic is at work? Each of these three children has been at school for several months. Their comments indicate that they believe that reading is something that 'occurs'. 'You can read when you're six,' said Christopher recently. (Oliver earlier made this same prediction about his ability to tie his shoe-laces, using five as the key age. Sure enough, in the week after his fifth birthday, he was seen to be practising resolutely—with swift success, which did not seem to surprise him at all!)

We cannot know, with any certainty, what is going on in a child's mind, but it is a field of enquiry in which the parent can rival the expert. The opportunity to develop awareness, to observe children closely and sensitively, to relate what happens one day to what emerges as an utterance, or an action, the next day—or the next month—is the parent's priceless preserve. Insights, revelations, and mysteries come thick and fast at those parents who listen, look and reflect. (Child-watching beats bird-watching hands down, and you need never crawl out at dawn and risk a wet and muddy stomach . . . well, not often.)

What sort of stories will best nourish this burgeoning personality, then?

Almost all children, however inexperienced as listeners, will attend to realistic stories. Children of one's own age having fun, getting into trouble and bouncing back—here is drama indeed. And no one tells stories of everyday family life better than Astrid Lindgren.

The ups and downs and doings of small Lotta Marten, as recounted by slightly older Maria, with older-still Jonas, playing his mostly responsible part, make wonderful reading in *Lotta Leaves Home* and *The Mischievous Martens*. For good measure, their father sets an example of good-humoured parenthood which all fathers might use as a yardstick.

> 'Once when he came home,' (says Maria), 'we hid behind the coat rack and were very quiet, and Daddy said to Mother, "Where's all the noise around here? Are my children ill?"
>
> 'Then we jumped out from behind the coats, laughing.
>
> '"You mustn't frighten me like that," Daddy said. "There has to be a lot of crashing and banging when I come home, otherwise I get worried."'

The Marten children visit the dentist (where Lotta refuses to open her mouth), foist themselves upon kindly old Mrs Berg next door (where Lotta unravels the old lady's knitting and Jonas wins a leaning-out-of-the-window competition by falling right out) and go by train to stay with grandparents. Astrid Lindgren understands childhood profoundly; the three children's behaviour and escapades are always based solidly in child-nature. Many of their apparently funny remarks reveal keen perceptiveness, a quality often present in the comments of young children, if adults are prepared to listen. (When Lotta's cousin, Thomas, who is also staying at Grandmother's house, is afraid to sleep without the light on, his mother points out that at home he is never afraid of the dark. Lotta explains, 'At home it's his own dark, Aunt Katie. He isn't used to Grandmother's dark . . .')

There are also two excellent picture books about Lotta: *Lotta's Bike* and *Lotta's Christmas Surprise*. Ilon Wikland's illustrations, liberally sprinkled in black-and-white through the older books, and seen in bright primary colours in the picture books, are clear and expressive. One could not imagine Lotta without exactly these pictures.

Teddy Robinson must be met at five, if he has not been encountered earlier. He is a 'nice, big, comfortable, friendly teddy bear', who belongs to a little girl called Deborah. Things certainly *happen* to Teddy Robinson, but they are always visited upon him; never does he take action. Throughout his long catalogue of mishap, calamity, reversal, and modest victory, he remains an extension of his small owner, an owner whose spirit and imagination do nicely for the two of them, fortunately. You can *count* on Teddy Robinson, just as he counts on Deborah.

There are several titles available in a paperback edition, and two well-produced hardcovered 'omnibus' editions make splendid presents for the devotee.

Teddy Robinson's creator, his namesake Joan Robinson, is also responsible for the existence of Mary-Mary, a figure of classic proportion. Mary-Mary is a clear thinker and an honest practitioner. Here she is, making a cake, 'a nice raw cake', as she describes it, having decided that she prefers her cakes raw. This is, of course, an unofficial activity; but then Mary-Mary's doings invariably owe more to originality than to protocol. Two eggs in succession have just landed on the floor.

'Oh, well, eggs will be eggs, I suppose,' said Mary-Mary. 'It's no use getting annoyed because they're slippery. If I can't get the eggs to the cake, I shall have to take the cake to the eggs.'

So she did. She turned the bowl upside down and mixed the whole lot together on the floor. It was not

so good as a bowl, because there was nothing to keep
the mixture from spreading, but Mary-Mary walked
round and round, pushing it in from the edges with
the wooden spoon. It made the floor rather slippery
so she had to be careful where she trod.

Mary-Mary's long-suffering family are models of calm
resignation.

'My goodness!' said Martyn (confronted by Mary-
Mary's cake-making efforts) and he went away to
tell Miriam.
'You really are a *nuisance*, Mary-Mary,' said
Miriam, when she came in. 'Why can't you do
something nice and clean and quiet like everyone
else?'

Mary-Mary's ventures, however outrageous, are always
rewarded, quite unfairly, with success. She has a spectacular
quality which is seen in bold relief against the serenely
ordered backdrop of her everyday life. She appropriates—
from the dustbin—a disreputable handbag, which, in the
face of family threat of disposal, she keeps buried in the
sandpit. As necessary, she digs it up. The author's own
black-and-white illustrations for both Teddy Robinson and
Mary-Mary are lively and pertinent.

Milly-Molly-Mandy is not to be missed by the five-year-
old. There is honesty, energy and engaging detail in these
tales of small child activities. Against a nostalgically evoked
background, which has much to offer in its sheer freedom
from modern pace and stress, the small heroine and her
friends Billy Blunt, Little Friend Susan and Miss Muggin's
niece Jilly make their purposeful way through village and
field, exploiting to the full the resources of their idyllic
environment. Even the characters' names fascinate the five-
year-old. (Their influence was clearly present some years
ago in my eldest grandchild's list of her best friends:

'Heather-Next-Door, Simon-Down-the-Road and Bruce-Over-the-Bridge'.)

Lotta, Teddy Robinson, Mary-Mary and Milly-Molly-Mandy (and several others, such as Little Pete and Joe and Timothy, whose exploits are described in books listed at the end of this chapter) all have one chapter devoted to each of their adventures, a useful arrangement for reader and listener alike. Five-year-olds are not known for their patience, and a tale which starts and ends at a sitting may provide a more satisfying experience than an instalment.

Fortunately, there are some excellent collections of short stories available. Some five-year-olds will have met Sara and Stephen Corrin's *Stories for the Under-Fives*, and will now appreciate *Stories for Five-Year-Olds*. These are well-chosen anthologies, which dip into many of the established favourites (including several mentioned above) and also include lively retellings of traditional tales. Children love to meet well-known characters out of context; an isolated Teddy Robinson story will be welcomed as an old friend by the initiated, and serve to whet the appetite of newer readers. Never reject a collection because it has an already familiar story in it. You will be surprised at the reception your child will give to an old friend. And take note that *Stories for Five-Year-Olds* is the only current source of an incomparable story called 'The Little Boy and His House' by Stephen Bone and Mary Adshead—a story which, in its original picture book version, I was obliged to read aloud so often to a five-year-old son, that I finally knew it by heart!

Several excellent books for this age-group use the device of tying together separate stories by introducing a storyteller in the first chapter. Ruth Ainsworth (a name to be noted, in the literature for fives and sixes) uses such a plan in her *The Ten Tales of Shellover*. Shellover, the tortoise who lives in Mrs Candy's garden, sleeps for the winter and then wakes up to regale all the other animals, and Mrs Candy, with wonderful stories. In the main, these are stories about children; but children to whom astonishing things happen. Ruth

37

Ainsworth writes with warmth, humour and imagination. Her writing life has, so far, spanned more than forty years. She is an author who certainly *knows* how it feels to be five.

Some five-year-olds, of course, particularly the practised listeners, are ready for stories which proceed through whole books, each chapter dependent on what has gone before. Many such books are mentioned in the next, and succeeding, sections of this book. In the present chapter, I have confined myself to the needs of those children who are just developing their 'listening-without-looking' skills; though I believe that most five-year-olds, however experienced, would enjoy the titles mentioned or listed. There is a very wide area of overlap in my recommendations—and no rules at all. Your own experience will convince you of this!

Years ago I was looking for a ten-year-old son whose turn it was to dry the dishes, when our four-year-old said, 'Perhaps he's gone off to Narnia.' Somebody laughed, and she said indignantly, 'Well, there could be a magic wardrobe in our house. *There could be!*' Obviously, C. S. Lewis's book, *The Lion, the Witch and the Wardrobe*, at that time being read aloud to brothers of eight and ten, was making more sense than one might have imagined to their smallest sister.

Folk and fairy tales provide a fertile field in the search for stories which will capture and keep the attention of five-to-eight-year-olds. During this century, psychologists and others have attempted to explain the existence of myths and legends, folk and fairy tales, in terms which relate to the origins, growth and aspirations of humankind. There is little doubt that our fascination for such stories arises, in part at least, from their universality. We see our world, with all its truth and ugliness, its compassion and its violence, its wisdom and its stupidity, reflected in the myths and legends of every culture; and we see ourselves in the queens and the scullery maids, the princes and the woodcutters who people the folk and fairy tales.

The work of the scholars who study the old tales in the hope of uncovering evidence of their 'meaning' makes fascinating reading, and is available for those who are truly interested. But it need not concern us overmuch here. It is enough to know that the magic words 'Once upon a time . . .' will hold 'children from play, and old men from the chimney corner' as successfully today, as ever they did in the dim past. And we can demonstrate this to ourselves any time we choose.

The Fairy Tale Treasury, its thirty-two stories selected by Virginia Haviland and illustrated by Raymond Briggs, is probably the most beautifully produced collection available for young children today. Its large, picture book format makes it especially suitable for reading to a group of children, or as a present to a family. Raymond Briggs's pictures, in alternate double spreads of brilliant colour and black-and-white, are humorous or dramatic, friendly or frightening, as demanded by the flavour of the story. The retellings are consistently sound; Virginia Haviland has in some cases used existing versions of the tales from approved sources, and in others, retold the stories herself. This is an outstanding book, which can be owned and used for years, with confidence and pleasure.

At the Stroke of Midnight, subtitled *Traditional Fairy Tales Retold by Helen Cresswell*, is a favourite in my family. The size of a large novel, it is generously illustrated at every opening with either full-coloured pictures or black-and-white line drawings, the latter pleasantly enlivened with bluish watercolour. One might describe its twenty-four stories as the 'basic' tales. Helen Cresswell is an author of note, and has retold the stories herself; consequently, the collection has an evenness of tone which makes it totally reliable. (I was first made aware of this quality when, some years ago, one of my daughters, who was at that time teaching six-year-olds, told me that she kept *At the Stroke of Midnight* on her desk, for immediate access. She now has sons of seven and five and a daughter of three—and keeps it on her kitchen bench!)

Don't be put off by the term 'fairy tales'. You will find no gossamer-winged, namby-pamby creatures in these robust stories. In fact, with the exception of the odd evil, old woman or two (as, for example, the bad fairy whose pique at being excluded from the party led to the Sleeping Beauty's difficulties), you will find no fairies at all. Rather ogres, giants, wolves, bears, goblins and trolls make trouble for a succession of millers, queens, peasants and princes, with a generous sprinkling of third sons and spirited daughters. Your concern will be to preserve your five-year-old from the worst excesses of their hair-raising interactions!

I suggest treading warily, until you have established your child's resilience. But you may well be surprised. Psychologists tell us that all children have fears and fantasies which eclipse the contents of the most horrific tales, and that bringing these terrors out into the light of day to be shared (however scarily) with others, serves to reduce tension as well as to entertain. Certain it is that children love to hear these tales repeated, over and over again. One of my five-year-old grandchildren currently 'collects' versions of 'Hansel and Gretel'; he can never hear this story too often. Why? No one knows, but most of us can recall our own similar fixation with a story or book, or have seen evidence of it in our children.

Sadly, many parents reject the old fairy tales as unsuitable for modern children. Boys are reported (by mothers, in particular) as being 'only interested in space and cars'. A little probing usually reveals that these children have never actually *heard* 'Jack and the Beanstalk' or 'Rumpelstiltskin' read aloud by their own parents. Their acquaintance with these and other stories has been hit-and-miss, to say the least. Exposure to a well-told version soon gives the lie to parental belief about child preference! It is safe to say that no stories are more certain to succeed with children than the old, time-tested ones.

A word about 'versions'. Because copyright restrictions do not apply to the work of The Brothers Grimm and Hans Andersen, or to the many stories whose source is unknown, such material is often published in cheaply produced 'mass market' editions. Usually, these books have garish and trite illustrations, and one cannot count on the text to have that simple and pleasing flow which is the hallmark of the genuine fairy tale. Such books (along with comics and some of the 'series' paperbacks) do little harm, if children are exposed, also, to the 'real thing'. In fact, children start quite early to discern differences of quality, unconsciously preferring the best, if we help them to develop a sensitive palate for language—without divulging our intention, which might put them off entirely! It is as well, however, to get value for money when actually *buying* a book, and several easy rules of thumb will ensure this.

Make sure, to begin with, that the publisher has invoked the services of an editor, or collector, and that the sources of the tales, wherever possible, are given. This information will be printed on the title page, and possibly on the flap of the dust-jacket, or on the back cover. This is your guarantee that someone has taken care over this book. The price may be a little higher than that of the 'mass market' edition, but the worth will be there, if the editor has done his or her job responsibly. The name of a reputable publisher, again on the title page, and also on the spine, is an additional assurance of quality. You will soon start to recognize these once you are interested, and librarians and booksellers will certainly advise you, if consulted.

There have always been differences of opinion about the age at which children should be introduced to fairy stories. Often, of course, the decision is taken out of parental hands; the child hears a potentially frightening story read aloud by an adult at playgroup, or in a friend's house, or in his own, where it was intended for an older child. Often also, the young child surprises his parents by remaining undisturbed. There are as many reactions as there are children, in this field.

The arousal of fear, however, is not the only factor to be considered. Some of the best stories have complex and extended plots that make demands on both concentration and understanding which five- and six-year-olds may not be able to meet. It is hardly surprising that, in the face of such stories, they emerge believing that they 'don't like fairy stories'. The tragedy in this case lies not only in the child's present loss. There is a wealth of traditional material available for readers—and listeners—not merely of seven and eight, but of eleven and twelve and over, if the door is not closed by the use of over-difficult stories at an early stage.

(My youngest child kept me reading aloud to her until she was over thirteen—and, immersed as she was at other times in novels and text books, her choice for these sessions was always a fairy tale. And a son of fourteen, whose haversack I was reorganizing for a school camp, proved to have packed, as his weekend reading, the third volume of *The Lord of the Rings*, an indescribably sexy-looking paperback—and Andrew Lang's old *Blue Fairy Book*!)

A point which is sometimes overlooked by those who fear to present fairy tales in which violent or frightening events occur is that, from a very early age, children seem to understand that such stories are at one remove from real life. Five-year-olds might well be expected to be terrified by a film which showed two modern children purposely abandoned by their parents in a forest, and shortly confronted by a wicked old woman who proposes to cook and eat them. However, the 'Once upon a time' formula seems to act as a buffer (even if the magic words are not actually uttered). How do children recognize the formula?

The secret lies, I think, in the unconscious identification of form. The typical, time-honoured opening (There was once . . ., Once upon a time . . ., Once, in a country far away . . .) is followed by the immediate introduction of characters, who just as quickly become involved in action.

> At the edge of a large forest there once lived a woodcutter with his wife and two children. The boy was called Hansel and the girl Gretel. They were always very poor and had little to live on. But at last

a terrible famine came to the land and the wood-
cutter could not even provide food for his family.
One night, he lay in bed, worrying over his troubles.
'What is to become of us?' he said to his wife. 'How
can we feed our poor children when we have nothing
for ourselves?'

'I'll tell you what,' she answered. 'Tomorrow
morning we will take the children out to the thickest
part of the forest . . .'

Place and time are not specified, and only Hansel and Gretel
are named. The characters are prototypes, the stepmother
cruel but strong, the father kind but weak. The children,
seemingly helpless, prove to be resourceful and brave—the
girl especially so. She it is who persuades the witch (totally
evil) to put her head into the oven which is being heated to
cook Hansel, thereby allowing Gretel to give her '. . . a push
that sent her headlong into the flames . . .'

It almost seems that children enter into a contract. 'Ter-
rify us temporarily, but let us know, by the flavour and
framework of the story, that all will be well in the end. Keep
it all a bit removed from modern life, and make the good
people good, and the bad people bad, so that we know where
we are.' (It is significant, I think, that few children notice the
weakness of the father in 'Hansel and Gretel'. He loves his
children, so he is good. Ambivalence towards a character is
out of the question.)

There is real wealth to be found in illustrated versions of
separate fairy tales. The above extract was taken from an
elegantly produced version of The Brothers Grimm story
'Hansel and Gretel', illustrated by Susan Jeffers. This artist's work has especial relevance for children; it is detailed
and yet miraculously clear, at once ethereal and earthy.

The homely warmth of Paul Galdone's work gives it a
suitability for this age-group which I believe puts it into a
class of its own. *The Little Girl and the Big Bear*, with text by
Joanna Galdone, is a case in point. The cover shows a huge,

lumbering bear, looking rather sheepish before the accusing finger of a confident, saucy small girl. Galdone's backgrounds commonly present European forests, complete with cosy huts and cottages—which, experience tells us, often house terrors within.

This example does not let us down. Nor does the little girl. (She is never named.) Lost in the woods and subsequently captured by the bear, she sees the good sense in obeying her captor (who is bumbling and bossy, rather than vicious) while she hatches a plot for escape. This involves hiding in a large basket concealed beneath a gift of tasty pies, which she cleverly persuades the bear to deliver to her grandparents. Every double spread in this satisfying book is designed with sensitivity and skill. The device of clothing the bear in a red military-style overcoat, complete with epaulettes and gold braid, gives almost every opening a splash of brilliant colour. Galdone's obvious preference for unsophisticated folk tales makes his illustrated retellings superbly suitable for five-year-olds.

Picture books in every shape and size, and on every subject and level, are gobbled up by those five-year-olds who are lucky enough to encounter them. It is worth noting that many of the most successful picture books are written in language which is rich and complex. By contrast, many early novels use language which is over-simple and very unimaginative.

The shared enjoyment of such a book as *The Useless Donkeys* by Lydia Pender can be a richly rewarding experience for both reader and listener, combining as it does illustrations which are dramatic, original and colourful, and language which evokes both image and feeling.

> And still the water rose, filling the hollows and climbing the slopes, till the homestead hill was a round, green island, with the farmhouse perched on the top like a stranded ark. Father had brought his rowing boat, little by little, from the flats beside the

river, up the slant of the hill, and tied it fast to the
home-paddock fence.

But the donkeys? Where were the donkeys?

The speech of children whose literary bread and butter,
taken daily, consists of stories such as this one, reflects the
colour and drama of their experience. They are equipped,
not only for the prime tasks of expressing themselves and
forging relationships with others, but, in a practical sense,
for mastering the arts of reading and writing. They are
favoured children.

Picture books tumble thick and fast from the presses of
publishers, and there is wealth to be uncovered by the
discerning eye. But some of the best books are still the oldest.
No five-year-old (or six-, or seven-, or eight-year-old) should
be denied the joy of Edward Ardizzone's work. As I write, all
but one of the twelve titles which document the astounding
exploits of Tim, Lucy, Charlotte and their friends are still in
print, though the first, *Little Tim and the Brave Sea Captain*, is
almost fifty years old.

However, I see disturbing evidence that these incomparable stories are constantly passed over by adults, in favour of
more 'modern', often crude and spiritless, picture books.
Anyone who reads aloud often, and perceptively, to small
children knows that while bright colour may initially attract,
it is the story which renders the experience memorable, or
otherwise. Ardizzone's stories, reflected and extended by
illustrations which uniquely complement their spirit, trans-
port the child reader to another place and time; to a world in
which children are not helpless and subservient, but capable
and independent; a world in which dangers must be faced
and reversals accepted, before one can hope to return safely
to home and hearth.

In his more 'domestic' tales, Ardizzone's work has the
same realistic flavour. However improbable (and *Diana and
Her Rhinoceros* must surely be the least likely tale ever told)
one *believes* in these stories. Within their own framework they

have honesty and integrity. Diana does not consider deserting her rhinoceros, whom she loves with clear but undescribed devotion, any more than Sarah and Simon (in *Sarah and Simon and No Red Paint*) would swerve from the course of helping their penniless father buy the paints he needs to finish his masterpiece, and repulse the wolf from the family door. And Johnny the Clockmaker, resolute in the face of impatience and derision, stands staunchly beside Little Tim and Lucy, each of them involved in concerns which *matter*. Children do not deserve triviality or triteness in their books, and recognize quality almost unconsciously, given the opportunity. Books which have stood the test of time—as have the Little Tim tales, de Brunhoff's Babar the Little Elephant stories and Virginia Lee Burton's incomparable pair, *The Little House* and *Mike Mulligan and His Steam Shovel*— must be seen as classics in the making, and their omission from our children's lives a grievous loss.

What about poetry? If children have been exposed to nursery rhymes, jingles and simple poetry from earliest babyhood, they will be ready and eager now for stronger stuff. Quite apart from the benefits of language which is sharpened and tuned, the satisfactions of rhythm and rhyme and an early introduction to the experience of form, with all its appeal to the human ear and tongue, they will be learning to be literate; storing up patterns of language to draw on, when reading and writing appear. I say 'appear' rather than 'begin', intentionally. These skills 'begin', we now know, in earliest babyhood, with the first attempt to communicate, to receive messages from others. There is no such thing as 'starting to learn to read and write'; only starting to live.

Collecting your own set of poems is fun, and will certainly be appreciated by the child for whom you are doing the work. Include only poems which you have used successfully. A loose-leaf folder allows you to arrange and rearrange, to add and to subtract. My own collection, its earliest poems chosen and copied out well over thirty years ago, was published recently by Hodder and Stoughton under the title

For Me, Me, Me. On receiving his copy, one of our five-year-olds said doubtfully, 'It looks good, but I think I like the real book better.' The 'real' book is of course my old green folder, which has for years 'done the rounds' of grandchildren. But I think I know what he means; there is something personal and special about a handwritten book, especially when your cousins are next in line to borrow it! I, however, am pleased with the published volume, its modest 'Pooh Bear' style format fittingly housing eighty-nine poems which I *know* young children enjoy. Megan Gressor's spirited black-and-white line drawings extend, but do not dominate the poetry. I like to think of other families using this collection with pleasure, and I think that they will.

In *Babies Need Books* I recommended Louis Untermeyer's *The Golden Treasury of Poetry* as a 'family' anthology, and I reaffirm my faith in this splendid volume as a book to grow on. *The Faber Book of Nursery Verse* (mentioned in *Babies Need Books* as our family's source of Lear's 'A Was Once an Apple Pie') has reappeared, triumphantly, in paperback form, after an over-long absence, and can be just as heartily recommended. Here is treasure, indeed. According to the introduction, it is intended for children 'up to the age of about seven', but actually it offers a dazzling range of poetry for children several years beyond this level. Including limericks, riddles and jingles, there are over seven hundred poems between its covers: traditional and modern, familiar and less common, funny and serious. Barbara Ireson has edited both this book and *The Young Puffin Book of Verse*. Both might profitably be owned by teachers and parents.

The poetry collections so far described are 'print rather than picture' books, but there is a multitude of good poetry-picture books which can be used to woo the child whose experience of poetry has not been wide. Two splendid, comfortably small collections for this age are *Roger Was a Razor Fish* and *Days Are Where We Live*, both compiled by Jill Bennett. Each is well designed and easy to handle, the large, readable print arranged appropriately between Maureen

Roffey's clear-lined, colourful pictures. *Tiny Tim* is a slightly larger, more imposing volume than the pair just described, but Jill Bennett's choice of poems again assures a successful collection, with Helen Oxenbury's individual and expressive illustrations sealing the bargain.

'And "early readers"?' I can hear some parents ask. 'What of these? Surely five-year-olds, rising six, should be starting to read themselves?' I can hardly leave this chapter without touching on the subject, certainly.

It is my firm belief that a certain sort of 'early reader' has turned more children off reading—*real* reading—than it has ever drawn into the circle. I do not believe that we should worry about a young child's performance on text books, or lists of words. In fact, I believe that irreparable harm is done to some children at this stage by our insistence on such performance. This is a time when children's minds and imaginations are flowering and burgeoning in all directions at once, when they tend to ignore something quite 'simple' which we try to teach them, meanwhile mastering something much 'harder', smoothly, so that we may not even notice— or appreciate the accomplishment, if we do.

And only the strongest and most perceptive of us can leave well alone, at this stage! Learning as the result of *being taught* seems more valuable somehow. Success ought to involve effort, and if that effort is enforced by those in authority, so much the better. Our puritanical streak is just below the surface, when it comes to education.

Ideally we can leave 'graded material' to the schools, in the early stages (and hope that they keep it to an absolute minimum!). Nourishing children's minds is what matters— and what graded reader ever did this? Fortunately, there are several series of 'easy to read' books which contrive to combine some spirit with simplicity, and these may prove useful once a child is anxious to practise new-found fluency. But even these stories are greatly inferior, in imaginative and descriptive content, to the best picture books (and should *never* be used for reading aloud!). I have listed my choice of the best of these books in the next chapter.

As six draws near, schools—and parents—usually start to look for 'real progress' in the acquisition of reading skills. If they are dissatisfied with what they see, they sometimes start to apply pressure, achieving, all too often, quite the opposite result from that intended. Parents should be alert to this period as a 'danger spot'; a time when their children's cheerful expectation of becoming readers may falter.

Nothing works as well in this situation as good-humoured nonchalance about the whole topic—with a downturn in attention to the mechanical skills, and an upturn in attention to *real* books: books which will lift the spirit and set the imagination flowing.

Good books to look at, listen to and become part of: herein lies the cure for apprehension and self-doubt!

Book List I

Books to Use with Five-year-olds

Those titles which are mentioned in the previous chapter are marked with an asterisk (*). The name of the hardback publisher is given first in the brackets, followed by that of the paperback publisher, where there is one. Some of the books included in this, and the other lists, are no longer in print, but you should find copies in your local library. For the needs of very good listeners, consult further lists. The overlap is very wide, at this stage. Only a few picture books are included in this list. For a wider selection, refer to the 'Four to Six' chapter in *Babies Need Books*.

The Aardvark Who Wasn't Sure, The Cat Who Wanted to Go Home, The Gorilla Who Wanted to Grow Up, The Hen Who Wouldn't Give Up, The Otter Who Wanted to Know, The Owl Who Was Afraid of the Dark, Penguin's Progress all by Jill Tomlinson, illus. Joanne Cole (Methuen/Magnet paperback)

> There is a wealth of read-aloud material in these excellent books. The chapters are episodic, though each book moves towards a satisfactory conclusion. This device gives the listener, or reader, practice in attending to a long, on-going story, without too much 'carry-over' from chapter to chapter. The animal characters are lively and likeable, and yet keep faith with their species. They live animal, not human, lives, though their adventures are suitably exciting to hold the attention. There is much incidental, but accurate, information given about the life habits of each species, and yet no artificial 'teaching'.

**About Teddy Robinson, Dear Teddy Robinson, Keeping Up With Teddy Robinson, Teddy Robinson Himself* all by Joan Robinson (Puffin paperback)
**Teddy Robinson's First Omnibus* and *Teddy Robinson's Second Omnibus* both by Joan Robinson (Harrap)

The Adventures of Sam Pig Alison Uttley, illus. Francis Gower (Faber/Puffin paperback)
After more than forty years, little Sam, the youngest and most irresponsible of the four pigs who live with Brock the Badger, soldiers happily on. The veteran of innumerable homely campaigns, he is as engaging and irrepressible as ever. These are substantial stories; there is never anything trivial about Sam's doings, and five-year-olds must listen closely. Experience proves that they do, with Alison Uttley's timeless, simple and yet imaginative prose to weave the magic. A variety of titles.
The Sam Pig Storybook in hardcover is a joy to own, and is due for reprinting.

The Anita Hewett Animal Story Book illus. Margery Gill and Charlotte Hough (The Bodley Head/Puffin paperback)
Containing thirty-five stories about animals, this is a book to be acquired early, for it will last a long time— and in its new paperback format is very good value indeed. The tales are written in a straightforward, energetic style, which is nonetheless expressive, and easy to listen to. The depicted characters are real, live animals, but the effect is imaginative too, and the work of the two separate artists lends variety.

**At the Stroke of Midnight* Helen Cresswell, illus. Carolyn Dinan (Collins)

**Babar the Little Elephant books* Jean and Laurent de Brunhoff (Methuen/Methuen paperback)

51

Bad Boys ed. Eileen Colwell, illus. Hans Helweg and others (Viking Kestrel/Puffin paperback)
> This is a sound, if somewhat uneven, anthology, assembled by a well-known collector and storyteller. There is a range of levels among the twelve stories and poems; in fact, the collection will serve chilren well from five to eight, if parents and teachers take the trouble to read the tales ahead of time. Vicarious experience of other people's wickedness is always attractive, and most of the authors are well known in the field. 'A Picnic with the Aunts' by Ursula Moray Williams is both the last and the best story in the book, but should perhaps be kept until seven or eight. Adults may as well enjoy it in the meanwhile, however! Its flavour is delicious. And, if they decide to read it aloud, it will not matter in the least if its subtleties pass unappreciated for its action will delight. (This story was published in picture book format some years ago with wonderfully expressive illustrations by Faith Jaques. An old copy continues to delight my grandchildren—but the story is good enough to flourish alone.)

Boastful Rabbit Ruth Manning-Sanders, illus. James Hodgson (Methuen/Magnet paperback)
> Fifteen cheerful stories about Rabbit, who lives with his grandmother. Each is brief enough to use as a fill-in, when time is short and only a story will do. Ruth Manning-Sanders is an accomplished reteller whose tales have shape and vigour. The illustrations, in black-and-white, are agreeable and appropriate. A handy little book this, for either schoolroom or home. Also *Oh Really, Rabbit!*

A Book of Pig Tales ed. Rosemary Debnam, illus. David McKee (Kaye and Ward)
> These seven stories, four short poems and one long

story-poem (by Lewis Carroll), all of equal quality but wide variety, make a splendid volume. Only 'The Three Little Pigs' is familiar, and two of the tales provide tempting tastes of full-length books that may be sought out later (*Charlotte's Web* and *Dr Dolittle's Post Office*). For sheer, divergent lunacy, I commend to you the last story in the book, 'Mrs Simkin's Bed'. David McKee's pictures contribute more than mere illustration. They are generous, stylish and vital to the book's charm.

**Days Are Where We Live* compiled by Jill Bennett, illus. Maureen Roffey (The Bodley Head)

**Diana and Her Rhinoceros* Edward Ardizzone (The Bodley Head/Magnet paperback)

The Faber Book of Nursery Stories ed. Barbara Ireson, illus. Shirley Hughes (Faber/Faber paperback)
This is a superb, established collection of almost fifty stories. A broad range of authors is represented and the themes range widely. Shirley Hughes's comfortable but sensitive pictures make an exciting prospect of each page. A splendid book to dip into, constantly, throughout this whole period.

**The Faber Book of Nursery Verse* ed. Barbara Ireson, illus. George Adamson (Faber paperback)

**The Fairy Tale Treasury* ed. Virginia Haviland, illus. Raymond Briggs (Hamish Hamilton/Puffin)

Favourite Fairy Tales Told in England illus. Bettina and *Favourite Fairy Tales Told in Ireland* illus. Artur Marokvia both ed. Virginia Haviland (The Bodley Head)
These stoutly bound, well set-up volumes contain, respectively, six and five stories which are firmly based

in the folklore of their country of origin; they are all
potential 'favourites'. Virginia Haviland, an American
librarian of note, drew on established sources for her
material, but retold the tales with young children in
mind. First published almost a quarter of a century
ago, the collections have proven totally durable. The
print in each is especially clear, and extra space
between the lines makes the text itself less daunting to
'learning' readers. The illustrations are generously
placed throughout. Humorous or earthy, as the homely
nature of the tales requires, they are in each case
vigorous and fitting. Several additional titles in this
series are out of print—one hopes temporarily, as the
series is a superior one.

*For Me, Me, Me compiled by Dorothy Butler,
illus. Megan Gressor (Hodder & Stoughton)

Ginnie Ted Greenwood (Viking Kestrel/Fontana Lions
paperback)
   The large type and vigorous illustrations (by the
   author) will help to persuade potential readers that
   self-help is possible. And Ginnie herself—an intrepid
   female protagonist—will certainly entertain.

*The Golden Treasury of Poetry ed. Louis Untermeyer,
illus. Joan Walsh Anglund (Collins)

*Hansel and Gretel Susan Jeffers (Hamish Hamilton)

Hedgehog and Puppy Dog Tales Ruth Manning-Sanders,
illus. James Hodgson (Methuen/Magnet paperback)
   A book of seventeen stories, from the pen of a
   recognized authority in the field of folk and fairy tales.
   The stories come from all over the world, and range in
   length from two pages to nineteen; but their style is
   uniform. In all, animals interact lovingly, foolishly,

apprehensively and humorously, reflecting *human* behaviour in all its variety. On the surface, all is fun, and ends happily, with illustrations to match.

How the Whale Became and Other Stories Ted Hughes, illus. George Adamson (Puffin paperback)
A master of wordcraft has created, in modest format, a small classic. What made the various animals assume their own distinctive natures? All parents and teachers should have personal copies on hand for emergency use.

Jeremiah in the Dark Woods Janet and Allan Ahlberg (Viking Kestrel/Fontana Lions paperback)
'Once upon a time there were three bears, seven dwarfs, five gorillas, a frog prince, some sleeping beauties, a wolf, a dinosaur, a Mad Hatter, a steamboat, four firemen on a fire engine, a crocodile with a clock in it, a considerable number of giant beanstalks—and a little boy named Jeremiah Obadiah Jackanory Jones.' Pause, but only for breath. My generation would have described this as a ripsnorting yarn, and no better description springs to pen. Extensive colour at every second opening, with irresistible black-and-white between. Tongue-in-cheek nonsense, which positively romps along. Missing 'Jeremiah' at five constitutes deprivation.

Johnny Oswaldtwistle Kathleen Hersom, illus. Lesley Smith (Methuen)
A small boy does small-child things which can be counted on to appeal to five-year-old listeners. Modestly but caringly related; and how nice to have a small male to join Little Pete, Joe and Timothy. Almost all five-year-old activists seem to be female, these days! The illustrations support, and assist the new reader.

**Johnny the Clockmaker* Edward Ardizzone (Oxford/ Oxford paperback)

The Little Car Leila Berg, illus. Gerald Rose (Methuen/ Magnet paperback)
> This author has a feeling for children—and people generally—which shines through in all her books. Here, in eleven very short stories, she contrives to bring alive a little, old car as the central character, with his kind owner, a host of assorted other people and the odd animal supporting. Quite devoid of over-cleverness, in either language or situation, *The Little Car* is sure of a warm welcome from both girls and boys. Gerald Rose's lively illustrations splendidly capture the spirit of the stories.

**The Little Girl and the Big Bear* Joanna Galdone, illus. Paul Galdone (World's Work)

Little Grey Rabbit's Birthday Alison Uttley, illus. Margaret Tempest (Collins/Collins Cubs)
> One of the many enchanting stories in a series of little books which have arrested children's imaginations for several generations. A whole world of small field animals have adventures, and engage in country crafts and homely activities. Gentle concern for one another's lives pervades the stories, which demand sustained listening, for they are not short. Two beautiful, gift-style collections called *Little Grey Rabbit's Storybook* and *Little Grey Rabbit's Second Storybook* are volumes to be treasured. Margaret Tempest's superb, cameo-like artwork is here presented in generous whole-page pictures which truly grace these lovely books.

*The Little House Virginia Lee Burton (Faber/Faber paperback)

Little Pete Stories Leila Berg, illus. Peggy Fortnum
(Methuen/Magnet paperback)
> The note at the front of this book informs us that Pete
> is a 'tough, self-reliant little four-year-old', but no
> mention of age is made in the twelve stories that
> follow. This is fortunate, as these are tales for fives, as
> well as four-year-olds, to grow on; stories of an
> energetic little boy occupying himself in an ordinary
> but interesting way. Little Pete gets to know the people
> and pets in his neighbourhood, rides his tricycle, and
> on one very special day gets entangled with a circus
> elephant. Leila Berg's touch is light throughout, and
> there are six rhythmical poems on everyday topics, for
> good measure. Black-and-white line illustrations
> support, and do not dominate.

**Little Tim and the Brave Sea Captain* Edward Ardizzone
(Viking Kestrel/Puffin)

The Little Yellow Taxi and his Friends Ruth Ainsworth,
illus. Gary Inwood (Lutterworth)
> We learn that taxis, like people, vary in disposition as
> well as appearance, as we make the acquaintance of
> this spirited bunch. Cars are perennially popular as
> characters (see Leila Berg's *The Little Car*, in this list),
> and Ruth Ainsworth has a steady hand on the text.

**Lotta's Bike*, **Lotta's Christmas Surprise*, **Lotta Leaves Home*
and **The Mischievous Martens* all by Astrid Lindgren,
illus. Ilon Wikland (Methuen paperback)

Mary Kate and the Jumble Bear Helen Morgan,
illus. Shirley Hughes (Puffin paperback)
> Short, chapter-by-chapter stories about a small girl
> and her doings. Mary Kate herself is robust and
> enterprising. *Mary Kate and the School Bus* continues the
> homely saga.

Mary-Mary, More Mary-Mary and *Madam Mary-Mary*
all by Joan Robinson
Also available omnibus edition, *Mary-Mary Stories*
(Harrap)

Mike Mulligan and His Steam Shovel Virginia Lee Burton
(Faber/Puffin paperback)

*Milly-Molly-Mandy Stories, Further Doings of Milly-Molly-
Mandy, More of Milly-Molly-Mandy* and *Milly-Molly-Mandy
Again* all by Joyce Lankester Brisley (Harrap/Puffin
paperback)

The Oakapple Wood stories (Eight separate, small
volumes) Jenny Partridge (World's Work)
  Each of these truly beautiful little books bears the
  name of one of the inhabitants of Oakapple Wood: *Mr
  Squint, Colonel Grunt, Grandma Snuffles* and five others.
  The stories are agreeable rather than engrossing, but
  the lavish, enchanting pictures command attention
  from child and adult alike. The appearance of familiar
  characters in each tale can be guaranteed to appeal,
  and encourages cross-reference in the child who is
  lucky enough to have access to all the titles. There is a
  'Treasury' too, but it is splendid rather than engaging;
  in larger format, much of the appeal is lost.

Roger Was a Razor Fish compiled by Jill Bennett,
illus. Maureen Roffey (The Bodley Head/Scholastic
paperback)

Sarah and Simon and No Red Paint Edward Ardizzone
(Viking Kestrel)

Smiley Tiger Barbara Willard, illus. Laszlo Acs
(Julia MacRae)
  An example of the excellent Blackbird series. The clear

and attractive black-and-white pictures reveal that Ben
is about five. He is just a little scared of *big* things,
especially animals, but a holiday with his granny's old
friend, Mrs Merryfield, soon takes care of that. An
ideal read-aloud for five-year-olds—the author, as
most in this series, is a highly regarded novelist.

Stories for Five-Year-Olds and Other Young Readers and
Stories for the Under-Fives both ed. Stephen and Sara
Corrin, illus. Shirley Hughes (Faber/Puffin paperback)

Tales of Joe and Timothy Dorothy Edwards, illus. Reintje
Venema (Methuen/Magnet paperback)
These two little boys live 'in a big smoky city full of
houses and shops and factories, and streets where cars
and lorries and buses and motorbikes go up and down,
down and up all the time, and stations where trains
rush in and out day and night, and where there is
always noise, *noise*, NOISE.' They are both,
predictably, curious, inventive and high-spirited, as is
their friend Jessy, who lives in the same tall building.
All three are under school age, but this will merely
give the five-year-old listener cause for a little
superiority; their joys and worries are universal.
Expressive black-and-white line drawings reflect the
flavour of homely honesty. Also available: *Joe and
Timothy Together*.

The Ten Tales of Shellover Ruth Ainsworth, illus. Antony
Maitland (Deutsch/Puffin paperback)

Tiny Tim ed. Jill Bennett, illus. Helen Oxenbury
(Heinemann/Fontana Lions paperback)

To Read and To Tell Norah Montgomerie,
illus. Margery Gill (The Bodley Head)
This is a basic collection which will be tapped

hundreds of times between five and eight, if the book is owned; and this *is* a book for owning. The stories are of varying length, and are grouped usefully into six sections: First Tales to Tell, Stuff and Nonsense, Animal Fables, Stories Round the Year, Heroes and Heroines and Once Upon a Time. Modern, traditional, classical, humorous, serious, the tales provide a wonderful background for any child. Twenty years old, newly reissued, and likely to outlast the more flashy volumes by a century or more!

*_The Useless Donkeys_ Lydia Pender, illus. Judith Cowell (Methuen)

What Size is Andy? Moira Miller, illus. Doreen Caldwell (Methuen/Magnet paperback)
Eleven separate stories about Andy, the middle child of five, and his family. Cheerful, funny, loving stories of ordinary people doing ordinary things in individual ways which add up to happiness for them, and more than satisfying listening or reading for children. Doreen Caldwell's generously placed pictures are exactly right, detailed and yet clear, reflecting the warmth of the text exactly.

When a Goose Meets a Moose Chosen by Clare Scott-Mitchell, illus. Louise Hogan (Bell & Hyman)
A sumptuous volume which is picture book as well as poetry anthology, and is memorable on both counts. The range is quite wide: from a sprinkling of nursery rhymes to some eight-year-old poems. The collection will give good service for the whole of this period, once acquired. The illustrations are sensitive and expressive and do not intrude on the mood of the poems. The whole is a delight.

*_The Young Puffin Book of Verse_ compiled by Barbara Ireson, illus. Gioia Fiammenghi (Puffin paperback)

3

Six-Year-Olds
and Their Books

Turning six, with a year of school experience behind, brings a degree of surface competence which may mislead the observer. Six-year-olds have most of the disadvantages of five-year-olds, with a few of their own added, for good measure. In general, they assess themselves unrealistically; they *want* to be totally independent, and may appear to strain at parental ties. Actually, they haven't moved very far. Any sort of reversal brings the six-year-old scuttling back to the shelter of the family, as often as not in tears.

But on the surface, most of them are expansive. Hungry for fresh experiences, they look for new friends and situations. And they like to win. They are sure they are right, and cannot accept criticism. Opinions are in black-and-white, and the right is always with oneself, at six. Underneath are the doubts and fears of the year before; on top, an air of confidence which may range from the serene to the brash, depending on the child. Six-year-olds need just as much parental support as five-year-olds, but may lash out at adults who try to 'baby' them. Parents are no longer infallible, no longer the sole providers. A range of other people and services are becoming increasingly important.

The differences between children from favoured backgrounds and those from less adequate homes begin to show up even more strongly during this year. At the root of the contrast lies language; understood and spoken at first, with reading and writing playing an increasingly important role. Can there be any doubt that the child who has known books since birth, the child for whom the printed page has been a familiar source of delight, has an advantage? Fortunate children have, by this time, heard literally thousands of stories read aloud. Many of these will be loved books, repeated over and over again, a source of comfort, information and certain enjoyment in a life which at six becomes less and less predictable.

Such books should never be cast aside as babyish. We cannot assess their value, in any quantitative sense, but we know that old and loved books are as priceless, to their owners, as old and loved friends. Both are more important than ever before in these uncertain days. And, please, don't even consider giving away so-called outgrown books to younger friends and relations without the owner's permission! Any true book owner knows that books have other uses than merely to be *read*. Once loved, however long ago, a book never loses its identity. Parting with it is like cutting off a finger.

The six-year-old whose experience of listening to stories has been confined to school will almost certainly still have an underdeveloped capacity for sustained attention during read-aloud sessions. Teachers cannot be held responsible for this lack. Group listening is no substitute for the experience of warm involvement and intimacy which comes with family book-sharing. Ironically, children who have been reared on books in their own homes derive greatest benefit from school reading sessions, too. Unfair, but sadly true. Fortunately most children can be won over by a teacher who combines good humour and warmth with a wide experience of suitable stories, though the problem of matching book and child is a difficult one, if the range of experience in the class varies widely.

Where to start, then, with six-year-olds?

Once again, the documentation of ordinary, everyday events—with a dash of colour—is probably the safest starting-point. One can assume increasing maturity and willingness to listen with six-year-olds, but little can be taken for granted until individual children are known.

Astrid Lindgren again comes to the fore, with her Bullerby books. In this small Swedish village there are three farm-houses in a row. In them live six children—until Ollie's little sister Kerstin arrives to make seven, and add to everyone's fun. The stories are related by seven-year-old Lisa, but are excellent for reading to six-year-olds or younger children, if they are good listeners. In these engrossing tales of youthful activity and enterprise, adults support and, if need be, endure the enterprising and lively bunch, but never obtrude. These are real children, mercifully unencumbered with troubles more thorny than a loose tooth or a lost lamb, equipped with loving parents, securely established in a peaceful country setting. Ilon Wikland's black-and-white illustrations reflect the mood of the stories faithfully. Both text and pictures manage a wholesomeness which is never cloying, and which gives the stories enduring and comforting appeal. *All About the Bullerby Children*, an omnibus edition containing twenty-nine stories, is an outstanding gift book for any six-year-old.

The average six-year-old is ready for a short novel, and there are several titles which should not be missed at this stage. *The Bears on Hemlock Mountain* by Alice Dalgliesh was first published in 1952, and is as successful today as it was then. It is about Jonathan, who 'lived in a grey-stone farmhouse at the foot of Hemlock Mountain' and whose momentous adventure began when his mother asked him to make the journey over the mountain (which was really a hill) to fetch Aunt Emma's big iron pot. She needed it to make a 'good, big, hearty stew', with which to feed all their relations, who were coming for a small cousin's christening.

> 'Me?' said Jonathan. 'All alone? They say there are bears on Hemlock Mountain.'
> 'Stuff and nonsense,' said his mother.

But was it? Jonathan is despatched regardless. His subsequent adventures are simply related, with Helen Sewell's strongly drawn, woodcut-like illustrations in black, blue and white adding to the impact at every opening.

Jonathan's own repeated attempts to reassure himself soon have the listener as apprehensive as the traveller himself:

> THERE ARE NO BEARS ON HEMLOCK MOUNTAIN,
>   NO BEARS AT ALL
> OF COURSE THERE ARE NO BEARS
>   ON HEMLOCK MOUNTAIN,
> NO BEARS, NO BEARS, NO BEARS, NO BEARS AT
>   ALL.

Aunt Emma's iron pot is certainly big; big enough for a terrified small boy to take refuge beneath when the fears become reality. But were the bears real?

'Stuff and nonsense!' said Jonathan's father, despatched to find him by his frantic mother, and accompanied by a bevy of helpful uncles.

> 'But you are carrying your gun,' said Jonathan. 'So is Uncle . . .'
> 'Well . . .' said his father.

Drama indeed, with pace, colour and a strong central character to support.

Ursula Bear began her modest existence in 1977 and has, so far, not received the attention which is her due. Perhaps the reason relates to her inclusion in the unexciting-*looking* but actually valuable Gazelle series, published by Hamish Hamilton. Created (no other word will do) by Sheila Lavelle, Ursula begins life as a real child.

> Ursula was a little girl who liked bears. She liked big bears, small bears and middle-sized bears. She liked fat bears and thin bears. She liked tall bears and short bears. She liked furry bears and bare bears.
>   She liked the live bears in the zoo, the brown bears, the black bears, the koala bears, the honey

bears, the polar bears and the grizzly bears. Her favourite toy was an old teddy with no fur left called Fredbear. She only liked boys if they were called Rupert.

Ursula liked bears so much that she wanted to be one.

The account of Ursula's transformation into a bear is spellbinding, as are her adventures in her furry guise. That she is able to change back into a little girl adds fascination, but there is no 'Hey presto!' about the metamorphosis. It requires ingenuity and organization to change in either direction, and the procedures are fraught with difficulty and danger.

Thelma Lambert's line illustrations for the Ursula titles are endearing without being sentimental. Every opening has a picture of Ursula as either small cuddly bear or ordinary, if enterprising, little girl. Young listeners will surely turn into young readers with alacrity, in the face of clear but lively text, arresting action and expressive illustration.

As a source of sheer fun, not to mention action, suspense and wild exaggeration, the Laura books by Philippe Dumas are to be commended. The earnest improbability of these stories has shades of Edward Ardizzone; even the illustrations, while quite unlike Ardizzone's in detail, have a similarity in essence.

We are introduced to Laura in the first book, *Laura, Alice's New Puppy*. At this stage, she is '. . . soft and round, a furry black ball . . .', and Grandmother's warning that '. . . her present would get bigger as it was a Newfoundland dog . . .' goes largely unheeded. Not, however, for long. Any puppy's capacity to disrupt family life is prodigious, and Laura proves to have more than an everyday talent for creating chaos. Predictably, Alice's parents have been pushed to the very limit of their tolerance before Laura's more valuable capacities start to emerge. They manifest themselves first in the face of breath-taking danger to life and limb, as the children find themselves helplessly adrift on a stormy sea. The odds against survival are as monstrous as the seas, but Laura's courage and skill are greater than both. Her position in the family is cemented: we are ready for more adventures!

At the time of writing, there are three of these: *Laura and the Bandits*, *Laura Loses Her Head* and *Laura on the Road*. All four titles might be described as picture books; many pages have only one or two lines of text, and none has more than six. But they are longer than the average picture book, and smaller in format; clearly books for the sophisticated fives, sixes and sevens rather than for pre-schoolers.

The authors of both Ursula and Laura, in their own quite different and individual ways, illustrate an important quality in successful writing for this age-group. Neither author strains for humorous or dramatic effect, and in each series of books the text is direct and pointedly appropriate for that particular story. Achieving this sort of suitability does not mean that authors may not use their own individual style. In fact, it is *style* which gives life and virtuosity to a story—qualities which are sadly lacking when the text is 'graded', supposedly to make it easier to read. Such 'easy' text is often so vacuous that meaning simply does not emerge. Even at this early level, stories must flow and create their own climate if they are to become memorable; an essential feature of literature at all levels.

A short novel like *The Christmas Rocket* by Anne Molloy does more to demonstrate the difference between the trite and the condescending in novels for the young than any amount of description. In approximately three thousand words, the author makes us part of the life of Dino and his parents and grandfather, a family of potters in southern Italy. Dino has heard it said in their little village that his father is 'the finest pottery painter in all of Italy'. He is proud that at last he is old enough to help choose the best pieces to sell in the town; but sad, too, as their loved old donkey, Maria-Luisa, has died, and they must carry the pottery on their backs. This is Dino's first trip, and it is the day before

Christmas—'The Birthday', as they call it. They have already picked out the young donkey they will buy when they have saved enough money. Dino has chosen the donkey's name—Gian-Carlo—and they see him on their way down to the town.

> Usually Dino stopped to rub the donkey's furry back for a bit and to have a talk. Today, with pots to be sold he couldn't tarry but he did call out, 'Good morning, Gian-Carlo.' Then he said to Papa, 'Won't it be fine when we have enough money to buy all four of Gian-Carlo's legs at once?'
>
> Several times, Dino's family had saved enough to buy two of Gian-Carlo's legs and once they had enough for three legs. Then each time they had needed money for other things and had spent it. Each time that the money had been spent, Dino was afraid that someone else would buy all four legs of Gian-Carlo before they ever could.

All Christmas stories must have an ending which is more than just happy; triumph is required, for this most joyful of all seasons. The resolution of this family's immediate problem comes unexpectedly, but fairly, and Dino himself is the person whose kindness and energy bring it about. The warmth, honesty and triumph of this story make it notable.

When reading a story such as *The Christmas Rocket* aloud, it may be necessary to explain some unfamiliar references to the children as you go along. But it is desirable to keep such interruptions to a minimum. A story is meant to stand alone, and you can let it do so, usually, provided you have read it yourself beforehand. You might introduce it by saying, 'This is a story about a boy who lived in Italy,' and begin at once. Later, you might talk about the many beautiful old churches that there are in Italy, pointing out that there are different ways of being poor and rich. Dino may not have belonged to a family which had a car and modern electrical appliances in its home, but he was certainly rich in experience. Not only did his father create beautiful objects; he had also taught Dino to love and admire the old, faded paintings on the wall of their church.

Such a story can help children towards an understanding of other lifestyles and values. Too often, in our children's lives, wealth is equated with material possessions. The outcry for stories which mirror modern children's own experiences is an understandable one; but it is equally important for children to identify with other children in other times and places, to begin to accept and understand differences. We do not 'identify' with a character because he or she lives in a house like ours, wears clothes like ours, or is fat, or wears glasses, or has divorced parents or a handicapped brother. We identify if we feel a quickening of feeling between ourselves and a character—who may not be our own age, or sex, or colour, or even live in the same century as we do. Interest is aroused in another person's pursuits, enthusiasms and ambitions, however different from our own, if that person comes to life for us, between the covers of a book. To truly 'know' a fictional character is to have made a new friend. For the rest of our lives, this person is still part of us, long after the actual story is forgotten. But knowing involves feeling. To engender this feeling is the art of the true novelist.

A Box for Benny by Leila Berg has a magic which is hard to describe. For New Zealand children, Benny's world might almost be situated on another planet. With its total lack of grass and garden, its houses opening straight on to the street, where old newspapers tumble about, and '. . . cabbage leaves lifted their edges and flopped up and down', its cart-and-donkey ragman who, astonishingly, pays Benny with a red balloon when he produces an old jersey in which 'there was nearly as much mending as knitting', Fern Street, Benny's street, is unfamiliar, to say the least. But all children know about the seasonal passions—marbles, tops—and so the hazelnut game makes sense, even to those who have never seen a hazelnut. And Benny's urgent need for a shoebox to keep *his* hazelnuts in, if he is ever to graduate to the heights of player in the spring nut games, is a universal one: the need to join in, to be included with one's fellows in an accepted and familiar activity which is almost a ritual. It is the ragman's cheerful advice to a neighbour's child which starts Benny's magic. 'You keep on giving, love. And one day you'll get the thing you want.' But it is Leila Berg's knowledge of people, inside and out, old and young, which gives this book its flavour, an enduring quality which cuts across time and place, race and class. My youngest children had the original hardcovered book, published in 1958. Long lost, it has never been forgotten. I seized upon the Magnet paperback which appeared in 1983 with real pleasure, and then wondered what my grandchildren would make of it. I need not have worried. None of the magic has gone in the years between.

Children, and the adults who buy and borrow books for them, love series. It is easy to imagine that they find security in 'another Teddy Robinson, Milly-Molly-Mandy or Paddington'. We all know the feeling: a cosy, knowing-what-to-expect situation which reduces the demand on our mental resources! *The Incredible Adventures of Professor Branestawm* appeared in 1933, and was the first of a series of books about this engagingly eccentric inventor of astonishing contraptions. The early titles were aimed at children of about nine and over, and, relying as they did on comic spelling, outrageous manipulation of language and a somewhat localized English bureaucratic humour, had a restricted, if enthusiastic audience. Over the last few years, the absent-minded and entertaining old gentleman has been reissued in simpler form for the delectation of the six-to-eights. Still attended by his faithful, much put-upon housekeeper, Mrs Flittersnoop, and supported (misguidedly) by his old friend Colonel Dedshott, he can be enjoyed in all his dotty cheerfulness, embellished magnificently by Gerald Rose's splendid illustrations.

One almost feels that the Professor has been waiting all

these years for Gerald Rose's treatment, for it is inspired. The tales themselves are predictable in outcome—similarly catastrophic—but widely varied, from a motor-car which can be collapsed, folded up and stuffed into the pocket to a machine which produces any chosen hair-do (or six, simultaneously) at the flick of a switch. Any slight over-sophistication of text, which is brief, is more than compensated for by painstaking attention to detail in the pictures, which are generous—at least half the actual page area.

Six-year-olds are vastly amused by other people's discomfiture, provided all is well in the end. The indomitable Professor can be relied upon to come out on top (dishevelled, dazed but undaunted), and his enterprises are bizarre in the extreme. Little chance of successful imitation here—worse luck or thank Heaven, depending on your age and disposition!

I have left mention of A. A. Milne's Christopher Robin and Winnie-the-Pooh stories for this chapter, for I believe that for many, even most, modern children, six is the best age to encounter them. Despite the proliferation of editions—separate stories in single, small picture books, selections in 'deluxe' editions, fascinating miniature volumes tucked into tiny slip-cases, four to a box, even that ubiquitous emblem of the eighties, a pop-up book—there are actually only twenty stories: ten originally published in the first book, *Winnie-the-Pooh*, and ten in the second, *The House at Pooh Corner*.

These two collections are still my favourite forms of the incomparable stories, and I still believe that in their hard-covered editions, they are best of all. For these are tales which will be read again and again and again; and paper-backs do, in the end, give up the unequal struggle and collapse.

Why six as a starting-point? A. A. Milne's language has a quality of its own; solemn and yet light-hearted, formal and yet friendly. In part, it is the language of the English middle-class nursery of the nineteen-twenties, and as such is far-removed in flavour and idiom from the everyday speech of children in the electronic eighties. And yet it has its own logic and frame of reference, and this is quickly mastered by the young listener.

> Pooh went into a corner and tried saying 'Aha!' in that sort of voice. Sometimes it seemed to him that it did mean what Rabbit said, and sometimes it seemed to him that it didn't. 'I suppose it's just practice,' he thought. 'I wonder if Kanga will have to practise too so as to understand it.'

In fact, the opportunity to become part of the well-defined world of Christopher Robin, Pooh, Piglet, Rabbit, Eeyore and the others, if only by proxy, is a chance to be seized. It is quite common to hear children talking in the vernacular, once they are initiated—taking Strengthening Medicine like Roo, partaking of A Little Something like Pooh, mimicking Eeyore's gloom.

> 'Good morning, Little Piglet,' said Eeyore. 'If it *is* a good morning,' he said. 'Which I doubt,' said he. 'Not that it matters,' he said.

But the humour requires greater worldliness than three- or four-year-olds possess, though many children of that age listen with pleasure, missing the nuances but enjoying the action, the warmth and the recurring and dependable characters. The verses of Pooh, that beloved Bear of Little Brain, enliven and grace the stories, and are remembered long after the details of the tales fade. Any occasion calls for a 'hum' and these have style.

> It's very, very funny,
> 'Cos I *know* I had some honey;
> 'Cos it had a label on,
>   Saying HUNNY.
>
> A goloptious full-up pot too,
> And I don't know where it's got to,
> No, I don't know where it's gone—
>   Well, it's funny.

'What's "goloptious" mean?' asked one of our five-year-olds when I was reading 'Piglet Meets a Heffalump' recently. 'Yummy,' said her seven-year-old brother quickly, so as not to interrupt the story. I feel sure that Christopher Milne was not familiar with 'yummy', but it did nicely. Language changes, but not the fundamentals enshrined by it.

Some years ago, when a week of cold and rain kept my family inside the beach cottage we had rented for our holidays, I read (with help from the oldest children) all of the stories to a mixed audience of three- to fifteen-year-olds. Again, Christopher Robin, Pooh Bear, Piglet and the others stood the test. And once, when our youngest daughter, then thirteen, returned from a weekend with the family of a school friend and someone asked, 'What's her father like?', she answered, 'Well, he looks like Pooh and sounds like Eeyore,'—and we all understood without further description. When I later met this unsuspecting, aptly described man, I had difficulty in keeping my face straight!

The doings of *My Naughty Little Sister*, supposedly retold by an older sister of perhaps six or seven, can be relied upon to appeal this year. The stories extend through five separate collections, and spread into an omnibus collection and several small-format picture books. Because the viewpoint is the older child's, the stories strike a clear note. There is enjoyment to be had in the contemplation of four-year-old naughtiness, as well as smug satisfaction in knowing that *you* could not possibly do anything so silly. Dorothy Edwards handles this age-group with sure hands and heart.

Fortunately, the 'naughty little sister' herself is a spirited child and her escapades (wrecking a decorated trifle at a party while the 'nice children' all play Ring-a-Ring-O'-Roses, poking a stick up the chimney so that both she and her surroundings are enveloped in soot, and purposely disappearing at the fair, so that she has all the fun of being brought home in a police car) appeal also to boys. And, of course, she is supported, if not actively encouraged, by her friend Bad Harry, a small male of equally demoniac bent.

Big sister's overtly pious comments are wryly funny, and offer welcome opportunity for participation. 'I hope you aren't too shocked to hear any more?' is invariably received with a bellowed 'No!'—and 'Yes!' my grandchildren shout, when asked to vouch for the fact that *they* would not have done such a dreadful thing, would they? Black-and-white illustrations by Shirley Hughes catch the flavour with delicious accuracy, and the three picture books, with coloured pictures by the same illustrator, are a bonus.

And then, for the six-year-olds, there are fairy stories in all their fascinating glory. Perfectly possible, now, to cast a little caution to the winds; though some must certainly be kept in hand, or at least spread carefully rather than flung.

Wanda Gag's *Tales from Grimm*, first published in 1937, is a book to meet and savour this year, and to treasure for many to come. This author had peasant roots; her family had emigrated to America from Bohemia, and she was brought up on the old tales. The rhythms of the true storyteller, touches of sly peasant humour and a wholesome country warmth shine through her retellings and illuminate them.

Speaking of the right of all children to be nurtured on the 'customs, songs and folklore' of their heritage, Wanda Gag said, in 1939,

> In fact, I believe that it is just the modern children who need it, since their lives are already over-balanced on the side of steel and stone and machinery—and nowadays, one might well add, bombs, gas-masks and machine guns.

Today, we might delete several of these deterrents to child security—but think what we would be obliged to add! I believe, with Wanda Gag, that 'the good old tales' *can* provide an antidote to modern ills, and that all children have a right to hear them in their best available versions.

Wanda Gag's own black-and-white illustrations adorn this collection. To enjoy the fusion of text and picture here is to feel the relevance of the sturdy, well-designed illustrations to the earthy quality of the telling. Text, illustration and design together make such a satisfactory whole that one somehow knows that they have been arranged by the same person: a person of integrity, for story, picture and child have all been considered sensitively.

The sixteen stories contained in *Tales from Grimm* all have their roots in folk tradition; indeed, The Brothers Grimm themselves called their own collection 'Nursery and Household Tales', a more appropriate name for them actually than the 'Fairy Tales' they have become. Wanda Gag has chosen wisely, for these tales are uniformly simple. Even when an element of dread might be expected to intrude, as in 'Hansel and Gretel' and 'Rapunzel', the lightness of her style, with its spirited, economical use of words, takes us quickly to the happy ending.

> The Old One called and cried and frizzled and fried, but no one heard. That was the end of her, and who cares?

Far too jaunty a statement to allow horror to get a grip!

I have for many years used a wonderful collection of folk tales for this age-group, assembled by Leila Berg. My hardcovered copy is entitled *Folk Tales for Reading and Telling* and is precious because in this form it is now out of print. When I was sent a brightly covered little paperback called *Topsy Turvy Tales* by a publisher recently, I was delighted to see Leila Berg's name on the cover, and wondered what was within. Joy of joys! Only the cover has been changed, and that for the better; a coloured plate from the original edition, newly chosen, graces this new Magnet paperback. One can even accept the new title as being, perhaps, easier to identify and remember—and certainly appropriate.

I have always regarded the Introduction to the original edition as one of the best and most immediately persuasive statements ever made about storytelling and thought, sadly, that it had been omitted from the paperback edition. But it was my day for receiving presents! There it is, sensibly, at the end of the book, recast as an Author's Note, with not a word changed: a more strategic placing anyway. (A young reader may be disconcerted to find a wordy-looking Introduction or Preface at first opening a collection of folk tales—a truth I realized years ago when I found one of my children staring with incomprehension at such a page.)

Topsy Turvy Tales is worth acquiring for the Author's Note alone. But the eighteen stories, each equipped, in the Contents, with information about its country of origin *and* its telling-time (from four to ten minutes) will stand any parent or teacher in good stead, and any child in line for enjoyment. For these are truly folk tales; about people and animals, and their interaction with one another and with a range of mischievous, but *not* evil, little creatures, from the trolls in the Scandinavian story, 'The Big White Pussy Cat', to the Hobyahs of the English 'Little Dog Turpie', one of the fastest, most breath-taking and satisfying tales ever written. Leila Berg's version illustrates well the capacity of a story, which has rather horrifying features, to enchant, if it is told racily, in 'that warm, laughing way, that tells him that he and I are together on this, and we'll see the little old man and the little old woman and Little Dog Turpie safely through', to use the author's own words.

Stories for Six-Year-Olds by Sara and Stephen Corrin reveals the same quality of both choice and telling as the compilers' five-year-old selection. Indeed, the whole period under review—from five to eight—is very well served by these rich and rousing collections. There is no need to take overmuch notice of the specified age for each, though the upper levels may well require a listening fortitude which is beyond the average five- and six-year-old's capacity. Each includes in its title the words '. . . and other young readers', a fact which may be pointed out to the seven- or eight-year-old who feels demeaned by the 'six-year-old' implication.

Oddly enough, it is usually less capable children who object to such apparent slights. Accomplished readers enjoy, without shame or comment, the most elementary stories and poems, if they have merit. This is not surprising, of course; we are defensive at any age only if the situation is potentially threatening, as it certainly is to the older child who experiences the acute embarrassment of reading failure.

Although one need not adhere slavishly to suggested levels, the Corrins's collections provide parents with a good starting-point. The six-year-old anthology consists almost entirely of folk and fairy tales which, selected with a perceptive eye for the young listener's need for both magic and security, come with a guarantee of success. Shirley Hughes's black-and-white illustrations achieve a total integration with each story. Nothing ever jars, in the work of this fine and sensitive artist.

The number of picture book versions of individual folk and fairy tales available is dazing. As ever, one must take care to check on the retellings; too often, such books are bought by adults on the strength of beautiful illustrations, which may or may not reflect the flavour of the true tale, or speak directly to the child. I cannot stress too often that it is the story which will become part of the child, and be carried into adulthood as part of the imagination, however apparently 'forgotten' the details; a resource, as it were, part of a personal inner landscape into which all later impression is absorbed.

This being said, we must ensure also that the child's visual experience is a rewarding and nourishing one, and that a wide variety of illustration is encountered. Where we find integrity of text, spirit of retelling and appropriateness of illustration all together in a traditional picture book, there is richness indeed. Such a combination occurs in *The Three Golden Hairs*, a Brothers Grimm story retold by a master of the art, Naomi Lewis, and illustrated with delicate sensitivity by Françoise Trecy. The story of the Luck-Child, and the wicked king's attempts to get rid of him in order to thwart the prophecy that he will grow up to marry the king's own daughter, has a complex but easily followed plot. It observes the fairy tale conventions closely, but has an individuality which not only holds the interest intensely, but allows the artist considerable illustrative scope. The result is a book of brilliant beauty, a literary and artistic experience of lasting quality. Owning such a book might well make a difference to a child's life; a benefit out of all proportion to the cost, high though the price of hardcovered books seems these days. A thing of beauty to treasure is surely a child's right; and a book is not a static possession. A good picture book is an animate thing, different at each perusal, inexhaustible in its possibilities for discovery and pleasure.

Different in style, but of like magic is the Japanese story *The Crane's Reward*, translated from Miyoko Matsutani's text by Peggy Blakely, with pictures by Chihiro Iwasaki. The theme of the childless couple who gain, through their own kindness or charity, a child who is not truly human, only to lose that child in the end through their own failure to observe the conditions laid down, is a haunting one. Here, it is a poor Japanese couple who rescue a crane from a trap and are rewarded by the arrival of a mysterious and beautiful young girl. Their poverty is soon a thing of the past, as their adopted daughter is able to spin magnificent cloth which brings high prices in the market-place. But Tsuru-san has decreed that her parents must not try to watch her while she spins and in the end the old woman's curiosity gets the better of her, with predictable results. The illustrations have a balanced elegance; at once robust and dignified, sensitively tuned to the theme. This is a sad story, but it is devoid of any violence or even harshness. The old woman does not suffer from greed; merely an excess of curiosity. Six-year-olds are ready for an extension to their emotional landscape—and to yearn is certainly as human as to err.

Six-year-olds will continue to love the simple rhymes, jingles and poems which appealed to them in the preceding year and, with their increased attention span, listen with enthusiasm to more advanced forms of verse. As mentioned earlier, this is the age at which the differences between truly fortunate children and those whose needs are less well met really start to show up. And it is, of course, their understanding of language, with all its resource and possibility, that makes the difference. The evocation of true feeling is so *possible*, through the careful choice and presentation of poetry in the early years! One wonders why this aspect of poetry's usefulness has not been remarked upon by those who see it as their duty to instil in children, through the books they encounter, attitudes and beliefs about society and its prejudices.

Attitudes derive primarily from emotions; logical thought produces conclusions without necessarily changing feelings. We must somehow encourage children to adopt accepting attitudes to other races, age-groups, animals, the opposite sex; to think clearly and feel deeply in the problem areas which so concern us these days. Poetry, if it is good poetry, evokes feeling of every kind. Its potential for moulding attitude is considerable. Again, I suggest that parents, as well as teachers, keep abreast of their children's taste in poetry through the years by making their own collections of favourite poems. *I Will Build You a House*, published by Hodder and Stoughton, is my family's choice, from six years old and onwards through the years of childhood; a good start for your family, perhaps, but not as good as your own. I have included descriptions of other suitable collections in the lists for every age-group. And remember that poetry, more than any other literary form, is ageless. One *feels* a good poem— and no age has a monopoly on feeling.

Six-year-olds, probably more than fives, sevens or eights, are dazing in their differences, one from the other. Some of them, more especially those who have not enjoyed extensive listening and looking experiences in earlier days, still need very simple texts and frequent pictures. Others will listen attentively to long stories, or novels read several chapters at a time. But these differences are intellectual rather than emotional. I would not hurry six-year-olds on to levels of feeling and experience which are far beyond their capacity to absorb and understand.

In fact, this is a problem experienced often by the parents of very able readers. How does one reconcile high reading ability with the emotional immaturity which is an essential part of the young child's make-up? One of my daughters, currently faced with this problem in one of her children, said to me recently, with some despair, 'I suspect he is skating over the surface of much of what he reads. I know about the technique; I did it myself at his age.' It is not an easily resolved problem, but can be kept within bounds, if regular and informed help is offered to such children in their search for books. I will touch on the subject again in the chapter on eight-year-olds. By this time, the problem can be an obtrusive one.

As mentioned in the previous chapter, I have somewhat mixed feelings on the subject of those books which are commonly called 'easy' or 'early' readers. On the one hand, one must admit that success is all important, if children are to become enthusiastic readers. Just as certainly, however, I know that a great deal of such 'material' is so contrived and boring that its introduction puts potential readers off, at a stage when demonstration of the exciting nature of reading is all important.

This being said, I am prepared to give you my assessment of the series that are available. After all, we provide them for children's practice reading in our Reading Centre, and I keep the best of them in my private library.

The I Can Read books, published by World's Work, now number (with Early I Can Read books, which are rather simpler) over one hundred and fifty titles. They are, of course, not uniformly good, but it is safe to say that this series is a reliable one, and that some of the titles are excellent. Syd Hoff is well represented as an author, and one can count on his work for slapstick fun. Title Number One, *Little Bear* by Else Holmelund Minarik, would be a noteworthy book, in or out of any series, and the three following Little Bear titles keep up the standard. Maurice Sendak's illustrations certainly give superb support, but the stories in themselves are worth telling. They are funny, warm-hearted and varied in theme.

Similarly, Arnold Lobel's Frog and Toad tales manage to emerge as 'literature' rather than 'material' despite the constraints of the easy-reading form. This author–artist has an extraordinary talent for evoking personality in a pair of small, cold-blooded creatures, without abandoning their essentially animal natures. His illustrations capture homely interior, leafy countryside and quality of relationship equally, and make of these books small gems. Also illustrated by Arnold Lobel, and written by Mildred Myrick, *The Secret Three* is especially successful. It has everything: messages in bottles, a lighthouse, an easy code, 'mirror' writing, camping . . . and the most satisfying quality of warmth and friendliness.

Peggy Parish's *Amelia Bedelia*, that muddled but well-intentioned and lovable home help comes across well in this simple context, and Edith Thatcher Hurd's *Stop, Stop* and *Hurry, Hurry* were much loved by one of my own children. The themes of accident and catastrophe seem to suit the jerkiness of the very simple text.

I Can Read books cater widely, both for true early readers, and children of eight to ten whose reading capacity is lagging. The I Can Read Science, I Can Read History and I Can Read Mystery sections all include titles which appeal to older children, and are in no way demeaning. *Red Tag Comes Back*, *Hill of Fire* and *The Case of the Double Cross* are good examples.

I believe that the Beginner Book series, edited by Dr Seuss and published by Collins, has much to offer children who are just learning to read. Unfortunately, many children encounter these books in read-aloud situations long before school entry. A pity, I believe, for the mixture of jaunty phrase, rhyme and nonsensical situation, which is the trade-mark of this series, is a bonus for the very young learner. After years of almost constant publication, with new titles appearing regularly, two of the earliest titles still stand out:

Are You My Mother? for the real beginners and *Fish Out of Water* for the next age-group up.

One hardly expects a fresh and funny note to be struck in this field, but such an event did occur with the publication, several years ago, of Viking Kestrel's Happy Families series. Twelve titles, all by Allan Ahlberg, document the dotty doings of twelve separate families. Several different illustrators alike preserve the cheerful, energetic character of the text, and the stories are *real* stories; somehow, Ahlberg contrives to bring his characters alive, while still giving beginning readers plenty of support through repetition, simple vocabulary and short sentences. *Mr Biff the Boxer* is a favourite among our Reading Centre children—but then so are *Mrs Lather's Laundry* and *Mr and Mrs Hay the Horse*. There is not one title which does not work to keep the reader's interest and sense of humour active.

Bodley Beginners incorporate the work of a wide range of excellent authors and artists to achieve a series which has much to offer. This diversity is commendable. Too many series have a boring sameness, title after title. *Mrs Gaddy and the Ghost* by Wilson Gage stands out; and the sequel *The Crow and Mrs Gaddy* repeats the success, for which the artist Marylin Hafner must share part praise. *Leo and Emily*, from the pen of Franz Brandenberg, with his wife Aliki's engaging illustrations, concerns a spirited pair of friends with remarkably compliant parents, and Oliver Pig (from *Tales of Oliver Pig*) suffers the pangs of all small children obliged to cope with the intrusions of a smaller sibling. The gentleness and family warmth of the two collections of Oliver Pig stories remind one of Minarik's Little Bear tales, mentioned earlier.

Between this level and that for which the beginnings of true fluency is required—as, for example, by the Hamish Hamilton Gazelle and Antelope titles, and Julia MacRae's Blackbirds—there is a noticeable gap. Some children are by this time simply galloping along, and do not need special provision. Others require consolidation of skills and techniques, and find the transition to 'real' books difficult. Often, these children also lack the enthusiasm, or confidence to approach new titles. Heinemann's Banana Books are welcome additions to a rather under-supplied field: that which caters for the needs of such children, as well as supplying readable stories for younger, able readers. Many of these, while they may be reading competently, are still daunted by books which are complex in theme, over-long or densely packed with print. At the time of writing, there are six Banana Book titles, with promise of more to come. All are forty-two pages long, with coloured illustrations at every opening. The text is admirably clear, with generous space between the lines. The paper is of attractive quality, and each title is hardcovered. Of the first published Banana Books, *The Big Stink* by Sheila Lavelle (of Ursula Bear fame) and *Dragon Trouble* by Penelope Lively (an award-winning author for older children) are superior. But all will be enjoyed, I believe.

So, too, will Hamish Hamilton's Cartwheels, with their clear, readable text and colourful pictures. The first six titles show an agreeable diversity of background and theme, with Sheila Lavelle again represented as author, this time of a cheerful farce entitled *Harry's Aunt*. *Meeko and Mirabel* by Linda Allen is an endearing tale of two sea-going mice, and *The Ghost Ship* by Catherine Sefton involves small hero Bill in spooky but ultimately satisfying (if chaotic) adventures. True to their publisher's tradition, Cartwheels promise stylish writing, interesting stories and excellent production.

Jane's Amazing Woolly Jumper by Judith Hindley is one of the two first Polly and Jane titles to appear in Patrick Hardy's Best of Friends series. This is an 'easy reader' which is also a really good story. Jane confides to her school friend Polly that her gran is knitting her a jumper for her birthday. 'Nobody in the world will have one like it . . .' Jane is evasive, when Polly wants to come to her house to look at the jumper; there is only her gran there, until mum comes home, whereas Polly's house is full of cheerful family and animals. In the end, the jersey proves to be enormous, and Jane is appalled.

But Polly's imagination and friendly good sense turn the situation into a cheerful farce—and she comes to Jane's house, after all, and shares her birthday. This is a warm, funny story which will encourage children to practise new-found skills. Jill Bennett's colourful and expressive pictures enhance every page. A second Polly and Jane title, *Polly's Dance*, introduces Polly's brother, Thomas, and repeats the agreeable mixture of humour and warm-hearted family activity.

There are many more series available, and the point at which such writing merges into that with a specifically 'remedial' intention is hazy. A safe rule is that such material should always be seen as practice reading for children themselves. There is everything to be said against adults reading such stories aloud. Even the best of them are stilted and contrived, as compared with the books recommended in the body of this book, and in the booklists. The precious hours of story listening should be, for every child, a time of imaginative delight. This cannot be expected to arise from books where authors have felt constrained to count the words in sentences, the syllables in words, and apply rules for repetition and other techniques to their writing. Easy readers may well have a place in the lives of many young readers; but determined efforts should be made to keep them in it!

All things considered, six represents something of a plateau. Children have definitely moved on from baby- and toddlerhood, but have not yet felt the sharp nudge of expectation and demand which is to come—a good stage to capitalize on while it lasts, from a parent's point of view. A time to establish strong ties of affection, to share games and experiences, to enjoy a closeness which, in physical terms, will dissolve all too soon as independent childhood advances; and a time to consolidate books as indispensable tools for a full and rewarding life.

Book List 2

All About the Bullerby Children Astrid Lindgren,
illus. Ilon Wikland (Methuen)

The Amazing Koalas Peter Campbell (Methuen/Magnet
paperback)
   There are four stories in this rousing little volume.
   They document the doings of 'wicked Michael Wiley',
   and these are rich indeed. Each story features Fred
   and Stanley, small boys transparently disguised by the
   author as koalas, their unfailingly loving but extended
   father—and Michael Wiley. Michael is the sort of
   friend all children need; diabolical and inspired, he is a
   kind of 'other self', equipped with courage, invention
   and no conscience at all. Why are these small boys
   koala rather than human? To square with parents, I
   suspect. Some might fear that such example (very
   bad!) from real children would be sure to have effect. I
   have no theory as to why Mum doesn't appear. No one
   seems to need her, anyway.

Amelia Bedelia Peggy Parish, illus. Fritz Siebel
(World's Work)

Are You My Mother? P. D. Eastman (Collins/Collins
paperback)

The Bears on Hemlock Mountain Alice Dalgliesh,
illus. Helen Sewell (Puffin paperback)

The Big Stink Sheila Lavelle, illus. Lisa Kopper
(Heinemann)

*A Box for Benny Leila Berg, illus. Jillian Willett
(Hodder & Stoughton/Methuen paperback)

The Bus under the Leaves Margaret Mahy, illus. Margery
Gill (Dent/Puffin paperback)
> This is the story of Adam, who wishes he had a friend
> and finds first Mr John Miller (who proves to have
> just built a trolley against the imminent arrival of a
> young visitor, for a holiday) and then David, the
> young visitor himself. Mr John Miller bakes bread and
> fruit cake, makes his own ginger beer and, most
> exciting of all, has a variety of old rusty car parts,
> covered in creeper, in his back yard. Together, Adam
> and David unearth an old bus which, with help from
> Mr John Miller, they turn into a den. The book is full
> of glorious detail: painting, baking, learning to ride a
> horse and watching a tree-felling operation. Even more
> importantly, it is full of summer sunshine, fun and the
> warmth of a generous and original old man's
> understanding of young children. Margery Gill's
> illustrations are sensitive and expressive, in both mood
> and detail.

Captain Pugwash and the Fancy-dress Party John Ryan (The
Bodley Head/Puffin paperback)
> This, and several other titles (listed below), are 'easy-
> reading' stories about that well-known pirate Captain
> Pugwash (of picture book fame) and have been
> produced by their publisher in the same format as the
> Professor Branestawm titles described in the last
> chapter. They are all as racy and preposterous as one
> could wish, with illustrations to match. Other titles:
> *Captain Pugwash and the Mutiny*, *Captain Pugwash and the
> Midnight Feast* and *Captain Pugwash and the Wreckers*.

**The Case of the Double Cross* Crosby Bonsall (World's
Work)

**The Christmas Rocket* Anne Molloy, illus. Laszlo Acs
(Julia MacRae)

Cops and Robbers Janet and Allan Ahlberg (Heinemann/
Fontana Picture Lions)
> A small format picture book which will delight
> swaggering six-year-olds. The rhyming text is robust,
> and the coloured illustrations explicit and genuinely
> funny.

> This sneaking, creeping, fingering lot
> Would burgle a burglar, like as not
> This peg-legged, baby faced, villainous crew
> Would pick the pocket of a kangaroo.

> A wonderful gift for any six-year-old whose taste in books
> is not known; an irresistible little book.

**The Crane's Reward* Peggy Blakely, illus. Chihiro Iwasaki
(A. & C. Black)

Danny Fox David Thomson, illus. Gunvor Edwards
(Puffin paperback)
> For once, a fox's cunning is seen as the resourceful
> cleverness it actually is. Danny is an engaging fox
> whose determined efforts to help a beautiful princess
> are suitably rewarded in the end. Excellent read-aloud
> stuff.

**Days With Frog and Toad*, *Frog and Toad All Year*, *Frog and
Toad Are Friends*, *Frog and Toad Together* all by Arnold
Lobel (World's Work/Puffin paperback)

*Dragon Trouble Penelope Lively, illus. Valerie Littlewood
(Heinemann)

**Fish Out of Water* Helen Palmer, illus. P. D. Eastman
(Collins/Collins paperback)

*_The Ghost Ship_ Catherine Sefton, illus. Martin Ursell
(Hamish Hamilton)

The Gingerbread Rabbit Randall Jarrell, illus. Garth
Williams (Macmillan/Fontana Lions paperback)
  A gentle story about a mother who decides to make a
  surprise for her little girl, when she comes home from
  school. Inspired by meeting 'the biggest, brownest
  rabbit she had ever seen', she sets about making a
  gingerbread replica, only to lose him before he is ever
  baked, in the classic manner: he runs away into the
  forest. Loosely based on 'The Gingerbread Boy' story,
  this tale has a happier ending. The author was an
  American poet of note, and his text is beautifully
  written, without bulk or affectation. A comforting and
  yet exciting story, with numerous black-and-white
  illustrations by an artist of merit.

*_Harry's Aunt_ Sheila Lavelle, illus. Jo Davies (Hamish
Hamilton)

Helter Skelter: Stories for six-year-olds Pamẹla Oldfield (ed.),
illus. Linda Birch (Blackie/Knight paperback)
  Thirteen authors and poets are here represented, most
  of them established and some notable. There are
  altogether eleven stories and twelve poems, all likely to
  engage the attention and imagination of young
  children. A collection of this sort makes a good gift, if
  you are not sure of a child's interests. Here, the
  subjects range from a runaway steamroller, through
  several fantasies, to stories of modern-day children
  doing everyday things. The poetry is uniformly good—
  some funny, some haunting, all short and memorable.
  Black-and-white line illustrations break up the text
  pleasantly.

*_Hill of Fire_ Thomas P. Lewis, illus. Joan Sandin
(World's Work)

**Hurry, Hurry* Edith Thatcher Hurd, illus. Clement Hurd (World's Work)

**The Incredible Adventures of Professor Branestawm* Norman Hunter, illus. W. Heath Robinson (The Bodley Head/ Puffin paperback)

**I Will Build You a House* compiled by Dorothy Butler, illus. Megan Gressor (Hodder & Stoughton)

**Jane's Amazing Woolly Jumper* and **Polly's Dance* Judith Hindley, illus. Jill Bennett (Patrick Hardy)

*Julius and *Little Chief* Syd Hoff (World's Work)

A Kindle of Kittens by Rumer Godden,
illus. Lynne Byrnes (Macmillan)
This is a picture book for the experienced listener, for the text is full and descriptive. This author's assurance with language guarantees attention; there is no bulk, no contrivance, and the narrative flows. She-cat has four kittens and makes sensible arrangements for their adoption and upbringing. The old town of Rye offers a perfect background for the story, which is unsentimental and yet eloquently tender. The pictures glow; they are at once robust, and elegant.

**Laura, Alice's New Puppy*, **Laura and the Bandits*, **Laura Loses Her Head* and **Laura on the Road* all by Philippe Dumas (Gollancz/Fontana Lions paperback)

*Leo and Emily Franz Brandenberg, illus. Aliki (The Bodley Head)

A Lion in the Meadow and Five Other Favourites Margaret Mahy, various illustrators (Dent/Puffin paperback)
This useful and spirited collection comprises six stories

originally published as separate picture books: 'A Lion
in the Meadow', 'Sailor Jack and the Twenty
Orphans', 'The Little Witch', 'The Man Whose
Mother was a Pirate', 'The Boy with Two Shadows'
and 'Mrs Discombobulous'. Each is just right for
reading aloud; unlike some picture book authors,
Margaret Mahy writes stories which have lives of their
own, and do not need the embellishment of beautiful
pictures. Just as good: *Leaf Magic and Five Other
Favourites*, including, as well as the title story,
'Stepmother', 'Ultraviolet Catastrophe!', 'The Rare
Spotted Birthday Party', 'Rooms to Let' and 'Simon's
Witch Doctor'.

*_Little Bear, Little Bear's Friend, Little Bear's Visit_ and _Father
Bear Comes Home_ all by Else Holmelund Minarik, illus.
Maurice Sendak (World's Work/Puffin paperback)

Little Old Mrs Pepperpot Alf Prøysen, illus. Bjorn Berg
(Century Hutchinson/Puffin paperback)
Mrs Pepperpot has a problem: regularly, without
warning, she shrinks! Her plight is fraught with
difficulty and danger in her diminutive size, but there
is potential fun, and trickery too. Several more titles
chronicle her daily doings in one-sitting, chapter-long
tales. The cosy, expressive illustrations add charm.

The Lost Merbaby and The Wishing Nut Tree Margaret and
Mary Baker (Puffin paperback)
The first of these stories only just avoids toppling into
total sentimentality; but it does, and emerges as one of
the most enchanting 'sea child on land' stories
imaginable. The second tale is more conventionally
constituted, but together they make a splendid book.
The striking, silhouetted illustrations are very fine
indeed. The companion volume, *Black Cats and the Silver
Crown*, has the same clarity and old-style magic.

**Meeko and Mirabel* Linda Allen, illus. Linda Birch
(Hamish Hamilton)

**Mr and Mrs Hay the Horse* illus. Colin McNaughton,
**Mr Biff the Boxer* illus. Janet Ahlberg and **Mrs Lather's
Laundry* illus. André Amstutz all by Allan Ahlberg
(Viking Kestrel/Puffin paperback)

**Mrs Gaddy and the Ghost* and **The Crow and Mrs Gaddy*
Wilson Gage, illus. Marylin Hafner (The Bodley Head/
Scholastic paperback)

**My Naughty Little Sister, My Naughty Little Sister's Friends,
More Naughty Little Sister Stories, When My Naughty Little
Sister Was Good* and *My Naughty Little Sister and Bad
Harry* all by Dorothy Edwards, illus. Shirley Hughes
Also available: omnibus edition, *All About My Naughty
Little Sister*, and three picture books, *My Naughty Little
Sister Goes Fishing, My Naughty Little Sister and Bad Harry's
Rabbit* and *My Naughty Little Sister at the Fair* (Methuen/
Magnet paperback)

A Necklace of Raindrops Joan Aiken, illus. Jan
Pienkowski (Cape/Puffin paperback)
  The eight stories in this outstanding book have an air
  of everyday ordinariness, mixed up with out-of-this-
  world magic which can be relied upon to enthral. Six-
  year-olds still half believe that there might be

  . . . elves in the shelves
      mermaids in the bathtub
        penguins in the ice box
          rabbits in the coal-bin
            peacocks on the table and
              seals in the sink . . .

Helping them to believe a little longer will do no harm.

Pienkowski's illustrations extend the magic. The hard-covered edition has eight full-page, coloured illustrations, one to each tale, with black-and-white silhouettes at almost every opening. The print is generously large; the whole, a special book which makes a wonderful present. The paperback edition preserves this quality as well as its reduced size allows, but the original is incomparable, and worth the higher price. *Tale of a One-Way Street*, by the same author and artist team, repeats the formula with equal success.

The New Golden Land Anthology ed. Judith Elkin, illus. Vanessa Julian-Ottie and others (Viking Kestrel/ Puffin paperback)

James Reeves edited the original from which this stout and tempting volume derived. Its title *A Golden Land* so purely described the earlier anthology's nature that owners of the dear old book may disapprove of the modern version. They will not disapprove of the book itself, however, either of its splendidly compelling dust-jacket and fitting black-and-white illustrations, or of the feast of 'Stories, Poems, Songs, New and Old', which its title page accurately assures us it contains. The modern additions give it a present-day touch, and the original character has been carefully preserved; it looks and feels like its predecessor. (Such a book may seem expensive, but no more than six separate paperbacks could be purchased for the same price. And this is a huge, beautifully presented and hardcovered book; an insurance against months and years of 'Read me a story!' requests.)

Oh, Abigail! Moira Miller, illus. Doreen Caldwell (Methuen/Magnet paperback)

The keynote of Abigail's family is informality, of a warm and cheerful kind. The parents' mode of speech mirrors the mood of good-humoured exasperation

which Abigail's behaviour understandably arouses.
'Well go on!' yelled Mum. 'Get it sorted out before I
dump the lot in the bin!' The stories are entertaining,
and Abigail, her brother Paul and Mum and Dad all
come alive as the spirited and caring lot that they are.
Doreen Caldwell's black-and-white illustrations are
exceptionally good; detailed, but clear-lined, well
designed and executed. A second volume, *Just Like
Abigail*, carries on the tradition.

Once Upon a Rhyme: 101 Poems for Young Children ed. Sara
and Stephen Corrin, illus. Jill Bennett (Faber/Puffin
paperback)
Beautifully presented, with eye-catching dust-jacket,
generous arrangement of poems set in clear type, and
black-and-white illustrations which are robust and yet
imaginative, this is an outstanding book. Eight full-
page, coloured illustrations evoke the 'plates' of days
gone by and make the book itself especially suitable to
give as a present. The selection will not disappoint; the
poetry ranges widely, but favours a rousing-to-
humorous note which is bound to appeal to six-year-
olds, and will be enjoyed for several years.

*Professor Branestawm and the Wild Letters, *Professor
Branestawm's Building Bust-up*, *Professor Branestawm's
Crunchy Crockery*, *Professor Branestawm's Hair-Raising Idea*,
Professor Branestawm's Mouse War and *Professor
Branestawm's Pocket Motor Car* all by Norman Hunter,
illus. Gerald Rose (The Bodley Head/Puffin paperback)

The Rainy Picnic and Outing for Three Pamela Rogers, illus.
Priscilla Clive (Puffin paperback)
Each of these excellent stories occupies half of the book
in this generously illustrated, large-print volume of
modest but certain quality. In the first, Michael is
justifiably annoyed when a promised picnic is rendered

doubly impossible: it is pouring with rain, and the
baby is not well. Only the arrival of Aunt Em—
redoubtable, bossy, *inspired* Aunt Em—saves the day.
In the second story, Michael and Aunt Em—by now
confirmed partners in joyful exploration—are obliged
to take Sarah, the baby, with them, as the children's
mother is ill. Michael, initially disgruntled, is bound to
admit in the end that this particular foray was a
winner! Each story positively pounds along, and is just
the right length for a read-aloud session.

Ramona the Pest Beverly Cleary, illus. Louis Darling
(Hamish Hamilton/Puffin paperback)
This author has a direct line to childhood which
astonishes while it delights. Ramona Quimby, her
older sister, Beatrice (Beezus), and their parents
conduct their lives in an ordinary house in an ordinary
American town without unlikely developments, but
with energy, warmth, good humour and a quality of
real-ness which never fails. We see ourselves in
Ramona, but also in Beezus, who, five years older, is
irritated by Ramona's pranks and her parents'
tendency to indulge her, but who is practical and
loving too. Beverly Cleary avoids the trap of over-
statement; she is not trying to prove anything, and
succeeds in creating real people.
    Henry Huggins, a contemporary of Beezus, also has
several titles in his own right. Again, they are
engrossing, often funny, and always wholesome.
    Other titles: *Beezus and Ramona, Ramona and her Father,
Ramona and her Mother, Ramona the Brave* and *Ramona
Quimby, Age 8.*
    Henry Huggins titles: *Henry and Beezus, Henry and the
Clubhouse* and *Henry and Ribsy.*

*Red Tag Comes Back Fred Phleger, illus. Arnold Lobel
(World's Work)

The Riverside Cat Pamela Oldfield, illus. Charlotte Voake
(Hamish Hamilton)

> Short and straightforward like its fellow Gazelles, this
> one tells of Steve's cat Becky, liked by all the boat-
> owners on the river except one: Old Bill. How Old Bill
> is won over is a warm-hearted story that will keep just-
> launched readers moving. Appropriate black-and-white
> illustrations help.

Satchkin Patchkin Helen Morgan, illus. Shirley Hughes
(Puffin paperback)

> Superbly satisfying stories of a little green magic man,
> who 'lived, like a leaf, in an apple tree'. The author
> has made no attempt to write simply. Her text is
> resonant and formal, but utterly compelling. Each
> separate story concerns Mother Farthing who lived in
> a cottage which was '. . . small and neat and smelling
> sweet of freshly baked cakes and pies'. But not all is
> peaceful; Jasper Dark, '. . . a lean man, a mean man, a
> man without a smile . . .', lives in the big house on the
> hill and is a threat to all peaceful life around him. But
> Satchkin Patchkin's ways are ingenious and Mother
> Farthing's heart is strong . . . Shirley Hughes handles
> cottage, countryside and characters with skill and
> sensitivity, in the accompanying black-and-white
> illustrations. A sequel, *Mother Farthing's Luck*, preserves
> the magic.

*The Secret Three Mildred Myrick, illus. Arnold Lobel
(World's Work)

Spring Story, *Summer Story*, *Autumn Story* and *Winter Story* all
by Jill Barklem (Collins)

> These four small squarish books are notable more for
> their exquisite appearance, and the almost breath-
> taking beauty of their delicate and detailed illustrations
> than for any excellence of plot. However,

characterization is sound, the families of mice which
inhabit Brambly Hedge interacting busily in their
endless preparation and storing of food, with plenty of
treats and celebrations to add colour to life—and an
occasional crisis to liven things up. This series has the
same 'collection' value as the Oakapple Wood books
(see Five-year-old list).

Stop, Stop Edith Thatcher Hurd, illus. Clement Hurd
(World's Work)

Stories for Six-Year-Olds and Other Young Readers Sara and
Stephen Corrin, illus. Shirley Hughes (Faber/Puffin
paperback)

Tales for Telling Leila Berg, illus. Danuta Laskowska
(Methuen/Magnet paperback)
Seven stories, three from Haiti and one each from
Africa, Russia, Ireland and Poland, all told with this
author's characteristic swing and style. A useful piece
of information is the time each takes to read aloud;
from seven to twenty-eight minutes. 'This is a story
about . . . And this is the way *I* tell it,' begins each
story. One can feel the silence descending, as the
telling begins.

Tales from Grimm Wanda Gag (Faber/Faber paperback)

Tales of Oliver Pig Jean van Leeuwen, illus. Arnold
Lobel (The Bodley Head/Fontana paperback)

Tell Them Again Tales Margaret Baker, illus. Mary
Baker (Hodder and Stoughton)
First published more than fifty years ago, this
collection is as fresh and full of charm as ever. Its
eighteen stories range from animal to traditional
themes, with a sprinkling of others beside, and are all

engrossing. Mary Baker's illustrations are lively and engaging. Some, in silhouette, are especially attractive.

*The Three Golden Hairs ed. Naomi Lewis, illus. Françoise Trecy (Century Hutchinson)

*Topsy Turvy Tales Leila Berg, illus. George Him (Methuen paperback)

Trouble for Trumpets Peter Cross and Peter Dallas-Smith, illus. Peter Cross (A. & C. Black)
This is a large format book of truly magnificent appearance. Each opening reveals not only whole-page illustrations which in themselves have startling beauty—magic, almost—but lesser pictures of intricate detail and interest, in dark blue line, as well as charts, maps, lists and embellishments too numerous to mention. The story, while it can hardly be described as a literary experience, is fast-moving, and so well supported by the visual effects that children are to be seen poring over each page, given the opportunity. And the theme, the struggle between the likeable Trumpets, who describe themselves as 'summer people', and the disagreeable Grumpets, 'winter people', who 'live in the dark, frozen mountains of the north, and are a sharp, pointed, cross-looking lot . . .' is a fashionable one, seldom presented as successfully as here to six- and seven-year-olds. The flavour is cheerful, even when danger looms. Both sides are comical, portly little creatures with teddy-bear overtones. Farce, rather than tragedy, is the keynote. A sequel, *Trumpets in Grumpetland*, seems to ensure the establishment of the species, and the series.

*Ursula Bear Sheila Lavelle, illus. Thelma Lambert (Hamish Hamilton/Beaver Books paperback)

Winnie-the-Pooh and *The House at Pooh Corner* A. A. Milne, illus. Ernest Shepard (Methuen/Methuen paperback)

4

Seven-Year-Olds and Their Books

'I thought that seven was big, but now *I'm* seven it seems quite small,' said my grandson, Thomas, last night. He was struggling into his pyjamas, his blond hair sticking up in damp spikes. He and his two younger sisters had just emerged from a bubble bath of snowstorm proportions. (A relation of some originality gave the three-year-old a gigantic bottle of the stuff for her birthday last week.) One might have imagined that Thomas would be in an ebullient rather than an introspective mood; he had shouted and splashed with the same reckless abandon as his sisters, only a few minutes before.

Perhaps the cares of the world are descending on his seven-year-old shoulders. After all, here he is, wrestling his own damp way into his pyjamas while both his sisters receive parental assistance. And the new little brother, lying on a rug on the floor, adored by all, might well be seen as yet another responsibility, however welcome. It is easy to feel inadequate in the face of hurdles that seem just a little too high. And eldest children are commonly of responsible, rather sober bent.

Tom's mother told me later that he had thrown himself on to the sofa the day before while the other children were outside playing and had complained that too much was being expected of him, at school and at home. Naturally, he didn't use those exact words, but his meaning was clear. One is moved to wonder how other, equally sensitive seven-year-olds cope with *their* lives. This child has parents who care about him deeply, support him when he is 'down' and help him to face challenges, as they arise. In addition, he attends a tiny community school where the children (seventeen, at the moment) are all known, and the teacher is both accepting and stimulating—a good friend rather than a master. And this child himself has considerable resources; a steadfast boy, I should call him, with a humorous twist to a nature which is naturally generous, and a perceptiveness beyond his years.

By seven, children are becoming conscious of the way they look to others. They are less likely to make scenes in public, though in the privacy of their own homes they may 'work off steam'—something we all do, if we feel secure enough, to the end of our lives. (Learning to do this so that our nearest and dearest understand our need, and offer support without themselves feeling threatened, is of course essential to mental health and it is a two-way affair. It doesn't work if one party is insecure, and it must be reciprocal.)

To the seven-year-old, it is a *one*-way affair; *he* expects and *you* give. But this should be, increasingly, more than a cuddle and the offer of food. Seven-year-olds respond, more and more readily, to our attempts to communicate with them, using language. We can open the way for them: 'You're really feeling worn-out and miserable, aren't you?' offers an opportunity for the child to fill in details. A sympathetic ear is far better than advice, at any age, and at this stage, may well provide clues about behind-the-scenes manipulations which are available to caring adults, and could help.

Seven-year-olds seem, on the whole, less spontaneously happy than six-year-olds. They are probably aware that the privileges of babyhood have finally been withdrawn, that more and more is being expected of them. 'Shades of the prison house begin to close . . .' said Wordsworth, and one imagines that he had seven-year-olds in mind. 'It's not fair!' seems to be the catch phrase this year—shouted by the assertive child, muttered by the meek! (No need to label; most of them swing between the two extremes.)

My own observation of seven-year-olds, our own and those in our Reading Centre, leads me to suspect that they are frequently over-tired. Certainly they look less robust at seven. Limbs have lost the touching roundness of earlier years, facial bones start to hint at their ultimate and individual form, eyes seem slightly duller, mouths inclined to droop. Seven-year-olds need unfailing background support, for their way is not smooth. Life has revealed itself as the burden it is to many of their elders. There is room for disillusionment; they have discovered that *their* needs are not, after all, paramount. Growing self-awareness starts to identify personal limitations and inadequacies which have not been sensed in the halcyon days of infant perfection. Disquieting sensations invade even the most confident breast.

There is evidence that the human intellect makes a strong surge forward this year. Impatience with younger sisters and brothers, anger at the teasing or advice of older family members, however well-intentioned, and frustration with personal incapacities are the by-products of this spurt, and lead often to trouble. Many of the most affected seven-year-olds are sensitive and intelligent children, ill-equipped by their sheer lack of experience for entanglement with life as it increasingly presents itself: demanding, relentless and difficult.

It is important to provide for fun, both rowdy and quiet, in the lives of such children. The growth spurt which ushers in the next stage will fortunately help to solve problems—and may leave parents wondering where their introspective son or daughter went, suddenly—but one must guard against the languishing sadness of seven. It is usually there, just beneath the surface, even in the most outgoing child.

Fortunately, effective counter-measures are available to adults who are sensitive to children's real needs. Enlightened teachers recommend occasional days off for weary seven-year-olds, and wise parents see the good sense of such breaks. In my own family I found that a short, unofficial absence was an excellent answer to those periods when everything seemed to be going wrong, for a particular child of *any* age. Giving one child his or her own special day of attention and mild indulgence while everyone else is at school or work does wonders for an exhausted spirit and tired body.

But isn't such special consideration likely to 'spoil' children—to give them the idea that we condone 'giving up' instead of 'pressing on' when the going gets tough? Not at all, unless school has been presented as a painful duty which must be endured, rather than a place where children are helped in positive ways to learn the skills they need to grow on. Children know, instinctively, when they need a break from an organized group situation. The gain is likely to be out of all proportion to the loss of a day's 'work' at school, for a child who is in no state to learn, anyway. (Actually, learning goes on constantly, regardless of what we do, or what we suppose the child to be doing—and what is learned at school and elsewhere often bears little relationship to what is 'taught'. In every field, at every stage, what is 'caught' is likely to be more important to true learning than what is taught—and here, parents are streets ahead of teachers in their potential to influence children.)

Sadly, in a family where all adults are absent from home each day, such a solution as proposed above may be impossible. The pace, mobility and expectations of modern life have a lot to answer for, in the lives of children. But all is never lost, regardless of circumstance, if goodwill, warmth and understanding are present in the minds and hearts of those people who are closest to children. If time is short, then it must be spent to best advantage. In particular, thought must be given to ways of cementing relationships.

Minute for minute and hour for hour, books offer the best rewards of all. Vicariously meeting characters of diverse type, race, period and age, sharing stories which may range from the mundane to the magic and from the funny to the frightening, gives parent and child something to carry together into other areas of shared experience. Doing the dishes, going shopping or fishing, flying a kite, putting up a tent or merely walking along the road together can assume a new proportion if you have also, together, been with Jonathan over Hemlock Mountain, plotted with She-cat for the safe dispersal of her kittens to good homes, or shouted with indulgent mirth at Piglet's terror on mistaking Pooh (his head stuck inadvertently in a honey pot) for the Heffalump they had plotted to catch.

> 'Help, help!' cried Piglet, 'a Heffalump, a Horrible Heffalump!' and he scampered off as hard as he could, still crying out, 'Help, help, a Herrible Hoffalump! Hoff, Hoff, a Hellible Horralump! Holl, Holl, a Hoffable Hellerump!'

A cry to be treasured for ever, boundlessly embellished, endlessly modified to the service of new situations!

Stories can be as complex, or as simple, as the child wants them, now. There will be times when old favourites, even dating back to pre-school days, are savoured; and, of course, most children will now be able to read these themselves. Such performances will give less confident readers much satisfaction and a helping hand in the right direction, as well as providing constant comfort. The warmth and security of loved old books is a joy experienced by too few human beings in these days of impermanence and change. Children who learn this are equipped with a priceless gift, that of knowing that old friends are there, for the turning of a page, that one need never be alone.

Predictably, nothing surpasses humour in its appeal to the seven-year-old, and this is a year when understanding of the way words work to produce funny results expands rapidly. Naturally, the well-equipped child fares better than the child whose language is unsophisticated in this field. But example bears fruit. Children quickly acquire the knack of riddles, puns, spoonerisms and other forms of the art, if they hear it practised at home and at school. We can certainly help, once we recognize the need.

Almost all children are conversant with the 'knock knock'

formula. Once mastered, they embellish it with gusto. The classic

> Knock knock!
> Who's there?
> Isabel.
> Isabel who?
> Isabel necessary on a bicycle!

will serve as example for endless experimentation, all of it requiring the young inventor to grapple with language and its fascinating ways.

Spoonerisms (named after a certain Reverend Spooner whose speech fell naturally, if regrettably, into this form) *are* funny, and much overlooked these days. As children, my generation cherished a few superb examples—'You are occupewing my pie,' 'Let me sew you to another sheet,' 'Riding along on a well-boiled icycle,'—and invented its own as well. These were pale shadows of the classics, but pleased us on wet days and during long evenings when we were obliged to make our own fun. Children today find spoonerisms just as entertaining, given opportunity and example.

The Ha Ha Bonk Book falls into a waiting slot this year and is one of the best books I know for encouraging reluctant seven-year-olds to read. The jokes are funny in the right way: plenty of play on words, with a dash of disrespect and lashings of slapstick imagery.

> What do you give a sick bird?
> Tweetment
>
> What do you give a sick pig?
> Oinkment
>
> Why does the ocean roar?
> Well, wouldn't you if you had crabs on your bottom?
>
> Doctor, doctor, my little boy's swallowed a bullet.
>   What shall I do?
> Well, for a start, don't point him at me.

A seven-year-old grandson trailed me around the house and finally out into the garden recently, reading random chunks of this valuable little book aloud. The jokes—even the hoary ones—are irresistible. We were both giggling helplessly before long. (What's bread? Raw toast.)

At its best, humorous writing has elements of both the slapstick and the subtle. The work of Hilaire Belloc, combining farce and mock tragedy with deft use of language, is especially suited to the needs of seven- and eight-year-olds. These children are only just emerging from their earlier state of total reliance upon, and belief in, the adults in their lives. Suddenly, they can risk a laugh-behind-the-hand at the posturing of parents and others. Hypocrisy and pomposity, once identified, become objects of shared mirth. Seven-year-olds close ranks a little among themselves, and start to feel better for this separation, however tentative. They can laugh with healthy disrespect at small Lord Lundy's grandmama who says, darkly, as he 'raises a terrible wail',

> 'Oh that I were Brisk and Spry
> To give him that for which to cry!'
> (An empty wish, alas! for she
> Was blind and nearly ninety-three.)

Lord Lundy's father's Elder Sister is relished as she confides to her Husband,

> 'Drat!
> The miserable Peevish Brat!
> Why don't they drown the Little Beast?'
> Suggestions which, to say the least,
> Are not what we expect to hear
> From Daughters of an English Peer.

Belloc's skill with rhyme and rhythm compels youthful attention. His *Cautionary Tales for Children*, first published in 1907, are full of out-of-date, Edwardian references, but carry the listener along, mysteriously producing meaning from material which many might regard as over-complex for this age-group. Children derive immense pleasure from Belloc's buffoonery—to have an adult on your side is too good to be true!

Of course, the 'tales' must be read aloud to the average child before they are tried alone, and this presupposes adult willingness to read and rehearse, ahead of time. The humour often depends on careful enunciation, but it is worth the effort. The art of dividing up long words in order to ensure rhyme and maintain rhythm will do no modern child any harm:

> A Trick that everyone abhors
> In Little Girls is slamming Doors.
> A Wealthy Banker's
> Little Daughter
> Who lived in Palace Green, Bayswater
> (By name Rebecca Offendort)
> Was given to this Furious Sport
> She would deliberately go
> And Slam the door like Billy-Ho!

Obviously, the word 'deliberately' achieves full effect only if pronounced syllable by syllable—'de-lib-er-ate-ly'. How many modern children are helped to experience the pointed pleasure of such satisfying phrases? And the delicious, tongue-in-cheek enjoyment of,

> When Help arrived, among the Dead
> Were
> Cousin Mary
> Little Fred
> The Footmen
> (both of them)
> The Groom,
> The man that cleaned the Billiard Room . . .

In case your seven-year-old starts to imagine that all poetry is old, get hold of a copy of Michael Rosen's *You Can't Catch Me!*. Embellished with Quentin Blake's illustrations—

which seem, sometimes, to reveal all and render words unnecessary—this is an engaging book. It will help children to see that poems need not rhyme; that their real function is to create pictures in the mind with the fewest possible words—which must, obviously, be chosen and grouped with deftness, imagination and precision, if they are to achieve this effect.

William Cole is a modern editor, whose collections of humorous verse are also well worth investigating. *Beastly Boys and Ghastly Girls* lives up to the promise of its title, as do *Oh How Silly!*, *Oh That's Ridiculous!* and several further volumes. Ogden Nash, Shel Silverstein and Spike Milligan are all represented in these collections, in all their delicious dottiness. Cole's anthologies are made even funnier by the brilliant addition of Tomi Ungerer's line drawings throughout. I can suggest no better present for a child, girl or boy, whose taste is unknown, than one of these splendid collections. Everyone likes funny verse.

And, of course, seven-year-olds must have levity in their *stories*, too, as an added antidote to possible depression. Pat Hutchins wrote *Follow That Bus!* for her son Morgan and his friends 'Dominic, Akbar, Jessica, Avril and the rest of Class 6', but she clearly had in mind all children who might ever embark on a school outing. Lucky Class 6! How many such expeditions have at their head a teacher of Miss Beaver's calibre? Agreeably absent-minded, cheerfully (if somewhat short-sightedly) undeterred by developments of an irregular nature, unjustifiably but lovably calm in the face of catastrophe . . . And how many drivers even start to compare with the zestful Mr Coatsworth? Handling his bus in an emergency like a star of the cinder track, enthusiastically involved (loving every minute of it, actually) to the farcical end . . .

This is a rollicking tale of mixed-up satchels, unlikely disguise and wild cross-country pursuit. The village policeman is classically ponderous and the crooks delightfully incompetent. No opportunity for slapstick is missed.

Accidentally (but hardly surprisingly), the chase is invaded by a whole tallyhooing hunt; the glorious finale has the entire cast on stage, banners flying.

Be prepared for protest if you try to break this story once you have read your way truly into it. I would choose a wet holiday and read the lot. Black-and-white illustrations by Laurence Hutchins uphold the farcical flavour and back up the text for the just-fluent reader.

Of course, humour need no longer be riotous. Seven-year-olds in their first stirrings of sophistication will enjoy a little deadpan fun. It is time for *Flat Stanley*.

Stanley Lambchop is an ordinary boy in a rather dull family, until the night a heavy bulletin board falls on him, and squashes him flat.

> 'Heavens!' said Mrs Lambchop.
> 'Gosh!' said Arthur. 'Stanley's flat!'
> 'As a pancake,' said Mr Lambchop . . .

The initial shock over, Stanley is hustled to the doctor where it is ascertained that he is perfectly well, if flat.

> Stanley was four feet tall, about a foot wide,
> and half an inch thick.

Mind-boggling possibilities present themselves. Squeezing under doors, or through the bars of a grating (to retrieve his mother's lost ring), are useful, if unspectacular feats. Being posted off to friends for a holiday in California '. . . with a great many stamps on the envelope to pay for both airmail and insurance . . .' is exciting, if a little dazing, and being flown as a kite by his brother Arthur, is exhilarating, dangerous and, in the event, almost disastrous. Of course in the end all is well. Stanley is reinflated (by practical Arthur, with a bicycle pump), and life for the Lambchop family resumes its even tenor. This is a delectable book for any age-group, ably reinforced by Tomi Ungerer's explicit black-and-white line drawings. A second title, *A Lamp for the*

Lambchops, seems likely to keep the family alive and vigorous for some time to come.

The search for realistic stories for the seven-year-old inevitably brings us to a consideration of the available series, among which Gazelles and Antelopes are probably the most firmly established. Both series cater, roughly, for the same age-group, but Antelopes are approximately three times as long as Gazelles (which series includes my own favourite Ursula stories). A decision to clothe these splendid little books in more colourful, less regimented covers has increased their appeal lately. Black-and-white line drawings serve both to break up the text and increase interest, and the themes are individual.

Published by Hamish Hamilton, these reliable miniature novels have been, in recent years, augmented by the arrival on the market of several other species, notably Blackbirds from Julia MacRae Books. This well-produced series includes *The Christmas Rocket*, described in the last chapter, as well as other stories which are remarkably well written, considering the limitations of vocabulary and situation imposed on their authors.

Read-Aloud books, published by Methuen, include the Lotta and Naughty Little Sister titles already mentioned, and many besides. Once again, the variety of established authors is impressive, their success in catering for the special needs of this age-group praiseworthy indeed.

It would be impossible to describe, let alone evaluate, each and every title among such series, but it is safe to say that the publishers mentioned above may be relied upon to produce books which are admirable in *intention*, if not always to the taste of particular children. Sustained contact with children and books will convince you, too, that only a very rare book indeed pleases *all* children. One of the most overlooked precepts in the reading field is that of personal preference. Children should be told that adults, too, sometimes abandon a book part way through as 'not my thing, really'. At the same time, they should receive encour-

agement to persevere with the first chapter of a recommended title in the hope that it may reach out and grab
them, given the chance. (They will do this all the more
willingly, if they are assured that giving up is not frowned on,
once an effort has been made.)

Parental previewing of such 'series' books at the library is
a help to some seven-year-olds, though others may regard
our well-meant intentions as intrusive. A few days ago a
seven-year-old grandson went happily home with *Little
Bear's Feather*, an Antelope by Evelyn Davies, after I had
skimmed through the first few pages aloud for him. Knowing
the child always helps, but only if we also know the book, and
this gentle but absorbing tale had been enjoyed by several
other children in the family. (Out of print, alas—try the
library!)

Peter Pan, 'The Boy Who Wouldn't Grow Up', sprang to
life as the leading character in J. M. Barrie's play of that
name in London, in 1904. Since that time the original play
has been performed innumerable times, and rewritten as a
story in many different editions. Curiously, Peter Pan and
his friend Wendy have almost become folk figures, many
people not realizing that they do not share their origins with
Tom Thumb, Cinderella and other characters from legend
and fairy tale. They have become household names, along
with Never-Never Land, Captain Hook and the pirates.
Their exploits make compulsive reading, and I believe that
seven is an optimum age for the experience.

Peter Pan and Wendy, retold by May Byron and illustrated
by Mabel Lucie Attwell, is a successful edition despite the
undoubted sentimentality of its text and pictures. To over-
earnest critics, at pains to point out regrettable aspects of the
story in weighty psychological terms (or even the aberrant
nature of its kindly but strange author), I say a curt 'too
bad'. The story is a glorious amalgam of all the themes which
ever held children spellbound. Within it, three ordinary
children—from an extraordinary household, where a Newfoundland dog rules the roost as nanny—are enticed away

by a magical boy with wings to a land of wonder and danger where pirates, Redskins, mermaids, lost children and a ticking crocodile play out their dangerous lives with swords and daggers among islands, caves, sailing ships and underground huts. What more could a reader or listener want? Future dreams and present games are fuelled by the page.

Indeed, once introduced to Peter Pan and Wendy, children invariably want to *play* it; to dress up, choose parts and begin. For it is all action of the most intriguing kind. One of my grandchildren *became* Peter Pan, and lived the part, night and day, for months. His mother was obliged to make him a Peter Pan costume, which was ultimately worn to a grubby shred. All visiting children were assigned roles—the text fortunately does not reveal how many lost boys, pirates, mermaids or Redskins were involved—and usually returned for more of the same, having caught something of the young director's fervour. Whether or not they had heard the story made little difference; Peter Pan proved infectious.

Margaret Mahy is an outstanding figure in the literature for this age-group, and, for once, the word 'literature' is justified. This writer's work covers a wide age range. There can surely be no other author who, already famous for a wealth of wonderful picture books and stories for the young, has gone on to twice win the Carnegie Medal—that coveted English award—with her novels for older children, *The Haunting* (1982) and *The Changeover* (1984).

One might devote a whole book to Margaret Mahy's capacity for true story-making and -telling, her warmth and humour, the richness and flow of her language, her almost miraculous insight into child nature and need. For our purposes, it is probably enough to say that modern children are fortunate indeed that her work is readily available, their parents and teachers equally blessed. For, in the read-aloud field, nothing succeeds like success!

How does Margaret Mahy achieve these wonders—for wonders they are—and still leave us feeling that the person telling the story is a flesh and blood, 'ordinary' person like ourselves? Because she *is*, and this comes through to children, I suspect. That Margaret Mahy combines this essence of true human-ness with qualities of imagination and vitality is part of her secret.

Describing her own feelings about children and books, Margaret Mahy says:

> A child's attitude to reading depends on its exposure to books and language in its home from the earliest years. I have an almost fanatical belief in the importance of reading aloud to children, so many of my stories are written with this intention.

One believes this, simply and absolutely.

Perhaps, from a young child's point of view, it is Margaret Mahy's capacity to intermix the mundane with the marvellous, without jar, which gives so many of her stories their peculiar wonder. Take the 'Aunt Nasty' story from her *Mahy Magic* collection, for example. Who else could arrange to have a real witch, who happened to be also an aunt, come to stay with an ordinary family, and have all turn out well in the end—with no one, least of all Aunt Nasty, diverging one iota, from his or her ordained role?

Just before she is due to leave (on her broomstick), Aunt Nasty discovers that the children and their father have forgotten the mother's birthday. In no time, she whips up a birthday feast of vast and wonderful proportions. But not with a mere wave of hand or wand; the children are requested to draw '. . . a birthday cake, jellies, little cakes, sandwiches, roast chickens, bottles of fizzy lemonade, balloons, crackers, pretty flowers, birds and butterflies . . . and presents, too.' These are then cooked to ashes in a saucepan, and the magic starts. The description of the party, all laid out, is masterly, and speaks directly to the child.

> All around the table were presents and crackers and balloons—so many of them they would have come up to your knees.

The children beg Aunt Nasty to stay, so that their mother can thank her.

> 'Certainly not!' said Aunt Nasty. 'I never ever say thank you myself. I don't expect anyone to say it to me. I love rudeness, but that is because I am a witch. You are not witches, so make sure you are polite to everybody.'

Several of Margaret Mahy's picture books (notably *The Dragon of an Ordinary Family* and *Rooms to Let*) speak most directly to children of six and over, for their language is rich and their plots complex. As a source of stories, three successive collections, called, in turn, *The First, Second* and *Third Margaret Mahy Story Books* provide a wealth of material, both everyday and fantastic—and mixed. Shirley Hughes has illustrated all three, and one cannot now imagine the procession of children, animals, kings and clowns which marches triumphantly through them, in any other guise. Both author and artist have total feeling for that earthy yet ethereal quality which is children's alone.

Margaret Mahy's work, at its most riotous or nonsensical, its most mystical and fantastic, or its most feet-on-the-ground, has an underlying gentleness, an acceptance and enjoyment of people as they are. Her stories are treasure indeed for the favoured children and adults who know them; good for heart and spirit as well as mind and imagination.

Seven-year-olds have been well served also by those astute collectors, Sara and Stephen Corrin, who have produced two volumes of stories for their enjoyment: *Stories for Seven-Year-Olds* and *More Stories for Seven-Year-Olds*. Again, each volume contains a feast of stories, mostly traditional, but with a sprinkling of the work of modern authors. Illustrations, again by Shirley Hughes, complement without dominating. Each Corrin collection from 'Fives' to 'Eights' can be recommended with confidence for its appropriate age-group. One can count on finding sustaining fare, tastefully presented, between its covers.

Between 1950 and 1971 eleven volumes about the doings of an energetic band of small creatures called Moomins appeared in English, translated from the Swedish. The seven-year-old who is reading well and likes something 'different' may well be overjoyed to make their acquaintance. This child is likely to be a potentially sophisticated reader; although the Moomins are tubby, genial little creatures, a strong flavour of Scandinavian folklore pervades the tales, and the characters are complex, and sometimes mystifying. They are wonderfully named. Beside Moominmamma and Moominpappa, there are Snufkin, Little My, the Groke, Snorkmaiden, Fillyjonk and a host of others. Personality and disposition are surprisingly well evoked, and relationships are real. *Finn Family Moomintroll* is a good starting-point, although all the stories are completely self-contained. Tove Jansson has created, in word and arresting illustration, a race of believable, if divergent, small creatures. She has done this with the sort of style, wit and humour which make the offerings of many modern authors seem brash and tasteless by comparison.

There is such a wealth of traditional material available to the sevens-and-up that suggestion of individual titles is difficult. It is time, however, for the introduction of reliable versions of both Andersen and Grimm. Companion volumes, both published by Gollancz, are my choice, the Andersen translated by Erik Haugaard, and the Grimm by Brian Alderson. In each case, the versions keep faith with the directness and vigour of the original stories. Each tale has been allotted one full colour plate by Michael Foreman, and each chapter heading a generous black-and-white illustration. These are beautiful, well-proportioned volumes to be kept and treasured.

It is relatively easy to find attractively illustrated collections of the stories of Hans Andersen and The Brothers Grimm, but more difficult to ensure that the text has been translated accurately and sensitively. Fortunately, some of the most reliable publishers have produced versions of one or the other—or both—and some of these are included in the booklists. And, of course, there is scope for personal taste. You will not be surprised to hear that I am currently reading aloud from an Andersen collection which contains 'Fourteen Classic Tales', faithfully translated by Stephen Corrin and illustrated by Edward Ardizzone. For me, this artist captures the 'novel setting and life of Andersen's stories supremely well.

For devotees of Maurice Sendak (of *Wild Things* fame) there is a neatly boxed two-volume Grimm with text by Lore Segal, which has rare charm if you like your Grimm in sombre peasant guise. Sendak's illustrations have an arresting power which fascinates, but will not be every child's choice. Wanda Gag's more jaunty retellings in her *Tales from Grimm*, mentioned in the last chapter, may still be the best choice for many seven-year-olds. 'Grimm', as has been pointed out before, 'can be grim.'

Picture book versions abound, and new artists constantly enter the field on the wings of established fairy tales. Some purists deplore this trend, reminding us that the old stories were meant to be told and heard, that the imagination of the listeners must be given free flow. I agree, but can still not regret the attentions of artists of sensitivity and skill to the work of the old bards and minstrels. And, whether we like it or not, the world has moved on. Ours is a visual society. Technology makes possible the presentation to ordinary people of a dazing range of art forms, through the medium of easily accessible books. I, for one, propose to go on enjoying, and sharing with children, the work of such artists in the fairy tale field, while still prizing my chosen 'collections' as major sources of Andersen, The Brothers Grimm and, later, The Arabian Nights, King Arthur and Robin Hood.

Once you have begun to take an interest in folk and fairy tales, you will notice that two names recur constantly as sources: Joseph Jacobs and Andrew Lang. These two men were contemporaries. Both born in the mid-nineteenth century, their combined contribution to English literature was considerable, though each is best remembered for his enthusiasm in collecting and retelling fairy and folk tales for children. Jacobs, although a scholar himself, made a point of telling his stories in a style he imagined a nurse might use when amusing her small charges, and this quality comes through in his *English Fairy Tales* and *More English Fairy Tales*. The Bodley Head has published a combined version of both collections under the title *English Fairy Tales*, and I cannot imagine a more useful or rewarding collection for teachers and parents to use with children between seven and twelve. A beautifully produced book with graceful but robust illustrations by Margery Gill, it contains no fewer than eighty-seven stories, including many well-known but not always easily located tales such as 'Cap o' Rushes', 'Titty Mouse and Tatty Mouse', 'Molly Whuppie', 'The Hobyahs' and countless others.

Andrew Lang's *Blue Fairy Book* appeared in 1889, and is probably his best-known collection of folk and fairy tales. But Lang's zest for his self-appointed task of collecting stories from all ages and places was boundless and led to the production of eleven more volumes. It says much for Lang's capacity as a storyteller that they are all still in print, and that almost every modern anthology includes one or more tales under his name.

A selection made from among the twelve Colour Fairy Books by the noted anthologist Kathleen Lines, entitled *Fifty Favourite Fairy Tales*, is an excellent starting-point. Margery Gill's black-and-white illustrations again grace the pages of this handsome book, which has recently been reissued by The Bodley Head. A newly designed dust-jacket strikes a dignified, magical note which transforms an established collection into a presentation volume.

New editions of the individual titles in the Colour Fairy Books series have been edited by Brian Alderson and published over the last ten years by Viking Kestrel. With their powerful black-and-white illustrations, these editions have breathed new life into old stories. Slight editorial changes have been made, but the tales are substantially intact. If schools could be persuaded to keep copies of these and the Joseph Jacobs's collection on a special shelf marked 'Compulsory Reading Aloud for Every Class', we might start to feel that we were returning to our children the heritage which is rightly theirs.

It is the universality of these tales which gives them their richness and quality, a truth which was brought home to me several years ago, when I helped choose books for a piece of research undertaken by the University of the South Pacific, in Suva. The project involved children who, speaking their tribal language at home, were obliged to learn English as a second language on entry to school. For the teaching of reading, the schools in the area had for some years used a basic word-by-word process, with predictably poor results. The research programme involved reading aloud daily to chosen classes for a period of months, from a wide variety of stimulating picture books. In these chosen classes, no other reading instruction was given while the experiment was in progress.

The results were startling in their affirmation of 'reading aloud' as the best 'teaching method'. The fortunate children who listened daily to stories made approximately twice the progress of those who continued with their formal reading instruction. And the most popular books? The traditional European fairy tales!

This is not surprising if you know something about the origins of all myth, legend and fairy tale. The patterns are there, in the lore of every culture: love, hate, greed, envy, kindness, cruelty, revenge, reconciliation . . . Such tales deal in basics. These Fijian children were used to listening to the stories of their own race, in their own homes. It was easy to slip into another language, if the same structure was there to support and encourage.

The legends of all cultures mingle and mix, themes occurring and recurring endlessly throughout. In my own country, New Zealand, traditional Maori tales bear a distinct likeness in form and theme to the legends of classical Greece—and there are said to be more than six hundred variants of the Cinderella story, occurring in almost every known culture! I believe that all youngsters everywhere should have access to their own and other races's folk tales, freely offered in the best editions, and told as they were intended to be. These old tales spark the imagination and nourish the spirit, revealing the common hopes, fears and needs of all humankind. That we neglect such a source in a world which is in desperate need of unity is, to say the least, short-sighted.

Public libraries provide a fund of good anthologies of fairy tales, folklore, myth and legend, many of them out of print and so unavailable for purchase. Exploring these makes excellent sense, for there is wealth indeed to be found in their ranks. A series published some years ago by Muller entitled 'Folk and Fairy Tales' provides a rich harvest of stories from almost every country in the world, suitable in both language and level for children of seven and over. Sadly out of print, it is still well represented in good libraries. (*Turkish Fairy Tales* is at this moment providing visiting grandchildren with a source of good stories in my house, and I am impressed all over again with the standard of both content and presentation in these fine collections.)

With eight approaching, established seven-year-olds are coming to terms with the vicissitudes of middle childhood, and managing their lives with less temerity and more confidence. Their increasing acceptance of their lot, while it induces an occasional stab of compassion in the hearts of the adults who love them, is converted increasingly into strength, if things are basically 'right'. Food, fresh air and fun, love, laughter and a chance to pursue the tantalizing answers . . . What more do you need, with an important birthday coming up?

Book List 3

Books to Use with Seven-year-olds

Adventures of the Little Wooden Horse Ursula Moray
Williams, illus. Peggy Fortnum (Puffin paperback)
  It is hard to describe the qualities which make this
  apparently simple, old-fashioned story superior;
  perhaps, even to identify them. But the tale will be
  remembered, long after it is told, and that is always a
  factor in literary excellence. The Little Wooden Horse
  is unlike any other toy Uncle Peter, the toymaker, has
  ever made. It can cry real tears, and talk; above all, it
  does not want to be sold! Man and toy become
  inseparable, and when poverty and illness overtake his
  master, the brave little horse sets out to earn money to
  help. His subsequent adventures are thrilling, but the
  Little Horse himself touches depths of feeling in the
  reader which are hard to explain. This is a long story,
  and yet may seem over-simple in subject to six- and
  seven-year-olds, while still a little daunting to read
  alone. Therefore, a read-aloud must!

*Ardizzone's Hans Andersen Stephen Corrin,
illus. Edward Ardizzone (Deutsch)

*Beastly Boys and Ghastly Girls ed. William Cole,
illus. Tomi Ungerer (Methuen/Methuen paperback)

The Beautiful Culpeppers Marion Upington,
illus. Louis Slobodkin (Harrap)
  A family of paper dolls, casually cut out by a small
  girl, prove to have an astonishing capacity for life, in
  this unusual book. The liberally sprinkled illustrations

are part of the secret; but the story is a certain success with both girls and boys.

The Birthday Mary Cockett, illus. Doreen Caldwell (Hodder & Stoughton)
A most successful early novel about a little girl who is hoping, desperately, that the new baby expected in her family will *not* be born on her birthday. Relationships are warm, and behaviour is believable. The illustrations, which are more than generous, provide interest and are in themselves realistic and attractive. This is a Stepping Stone book for young readers. Other titles are worth examining.

*Blue Fairy Book illus. John Lawrence, *Green Fairy Book* illus. Antony Maitland, *Pink Fairy Book* illus. Colin McNaughton, *Red Fairy Book* illus. Faith Jaques, *Yellow Fairy Book* illus. Erik Blegvad all by Andrew Lang, ed. Brian Alderson (Viking Kestrel)

*The Brothers Grimm: Popular Folk Tales Brian Alderson, illus. Michael Foreman (Gollancz)

Casey, the Utterly Impossible Horse Anita Feagles, illus. Roger Smith (Gollancz/Puffin paperback)
Finding a horse which can talk, and which wants you to be his 'pet boy' is fun at first for Mike, and for his sister Gloria, too. But neither of them, in the end, enjoys being enslaved by Casey's whims—or embarrassed by his antics. Funny, written simply and yet with style, this is a buoyant story which reads aloud well, and will attract some seven-year-olds to read for themselves. The pages are broken up with energetic, humorous line drawings, and the print is large and clear.

*Cautionary Tales for Children Hilaire Belloc, illus. B.T.B. and Nicolas Bentley (Duckworth)

Charlie, Emma and Alberic Margaret Greaves,
illus. Eileen Browne (Methuen/Magnet paperback)
   Unlikely pets—even ones which are invisible to all
   except their owners—are not unknown in children's
   literature. But Alberic, the dragon whom Charlie and
   his friend Emma discover in a hole in the road,
   deserves a place in seven-year-old reading. He is perky
   and engaging and transforms the humdrum lives of his
   two adoring friends. The illustrations are pleasantly
   complementary, and Alberic's adventures extend
   through two more titles, *Charlie, Emma and the Dragon
   Family* and *Charlie, Emma and the School Dragon*.

Country Tales to Tell Elizabeth Clark, illus. Cara Lockhart
Smith (Hodder & Stoughton/Piccolo paperback)
   Eight excellent tales for reading aloud throughout this
   period, and especially good for seven-year-olds who are
   reading alone—the print is very clear, and the stories
   themselves simply written, while well-rounded.
   Traditionally based, but often with an unexpected
   twist, they are sure to hold the attention. The pictures
   have both delicacy and vigour; they are enchanting.

David and His Grandfather Pamela Rogers,
illus. Janet Duchesne (Puffin paperback)
   There are three stories in this excellent book. All
   concern the doings and on-going relationship of the
   youngest and oldest members of the Jenkins household,
   both of whom are called David. The two share, also, a
   common problem, which Grandpa puts in a nutshell.
   'The trouble with us, my lad, is we're the wrong age.
   You—you're too young. I'm just too old.' However, as
   a team, they prove to be a formidable combination.
   There is a background of warm family life in these
   simple stories, and enough action and suspense to hold
   the interest. The print is exceptionally large and clear,
   and the line drawings faithful to the mood.

Did I Ever Tell You . . .? and *But That's Another Story . . .*
Iris Grender, illus. Tony Ross (Hodder & Stoughton/
Knight paperback)
> Two collections of hilarious stories about the narrator
> Rosemary and her brother Francis. The author has a
> subtle talent for creating humour which is
> simultaneously sophisticated and simple. The result
> may well be a convulsed adult, trying to get on with
> the story in the face of uproarious child mirth. Tony
> Ross's pictures are just right in flavour.

Dorrie and the Wizard's Spell Patricia Coombs (World's
Work/Puffin paperback)
> One of at least a dozen stories about Dorrie, the little
> witch 'whose hat is always crooked and whose socks
> never match'. These are domestic, chatty tales of mix-
> up and misadventure rather than supernatural goings-
> on, and provide wholesome 'filling' in the reading diet
> of newly fluent youngsters. They are unrewarding to
> read aloud, as the text tends to be jerky. Not to mind;
> the Dorrie fans will read them with pleasure and their
> heart is in the right place. The illustrations are superb,
> and are lavishly spread throughout each book.

The Dragon of an Ordinary Family Margaret Mahy,
illus. Helen Oxenbury (Heinemann)

The Dwarfs of Nosegay Paul Biegel, illus. Babs van Wely
(Blackie/Puffin paperback)
> Paul Biegel is an author of unusual skill, and this is
> apparent in his four books about the gentle but enter-
> prising band of dwarfs who live on a moor; '. . . not
> two of them, or even half a dozen, but at least a
> hundred, a whole race of dwarfs.' They are friends of
> the bees, who are the same size as themselves, and of
> the rabbits, who seem like elephants by contrast. Little
> Peter Nosegay's loved but feckless friend, Daphne the

butterfly, marries Jacob and leaves Peter to oversee the
hatching of her eggs into caterpillars, the retreat of the
caterpillars into chrysalises and their emergence as
butterflies ... an astonishingly moving metamorphosis,
in the event. The illustrations are perfect; they have
warmth without sentimentality. The hardcovered
versions warrant ownership.

Further titles: *The Fattest Dwarf of Nosegay*; *Virgil,
Nosegay and the Cakehunt*; *Virgil, Nosegay and the Hupmobile*
and *Virgil, Nosegay and the Wellington Boots*.

*_English Fairy Tales_ collected by Joseph Jacobs,
illus. Margery Gill (The Bodley Head)

Fairy Tales Terry Jones, illus. Michael Foreman
(Pavilion/Puffin paperback)
  There are thirty stories in this large, well-presented
  book, and each might be a traditional tale handed
  down through the centuries ... but is not. The author,
  himself widely versed in myth, legend and fairy tale,
  has used their conventions to produce new stories,
  which will delight. Michael Foreman's illustrations are
  alight with action, mystery and magic.

Fantastic Mr Fox Roald Dahl, illus. Jill Bennett
(Allen & Unwin/Puffin paperback)
  This is probably one of the most exciting books ever
  written. It is also frightening in the extreme, and not
  to be recommended for reading aloud to children
  under seven, unless they are known to be resilient in
  response to horror. For the three farmers' pursuit of
  the fox, his wife and four little foxes contains elements
  of real terror! In this story, the fox and his family are
  the 'goodies' and the three adult humans the 'baddies'
  —and suspense runs high before the tale is out.
  Exceptionally well illustrated.

*Fifty Favourite Fairy Tales ed. Kathleen Lines, illus. Margery Gill (The Bodley Head)

*Finn Family Moomintroll Tove Jansson (Puffin paperback)

*The First Margaret Mahy Story Book, **The Second Margaret Mahy Story Book*, **The Third Margaret Mahy Story Book* and **Mahy Magic* all by Margaret Mahy, illus. Shirley Hughes (Dent)

*Flat Stanley illus. Tomi Ungerer and **A Lamp for the Lambchops* illus. Quentin Blake, both by Jeff Brown (Methuen/Methuen paperback)

Fog Hounds, Wind Cat, Sea Mice Joan Aiken, illus. John Lawrence (Macmillan)
> This is an outstanding title in the useful and attractive Flying Carpets series. Joan Aiken's capacity for creating real magic in the lives of ordinary people has turned her collection of three stories into a gem. The series itself is welcome. There is some variation in quality among its titles, but all are worth looking at. They are encouraging rather than daunting books, with generous black-and-white illustrations at every opening, clear print, and extra space between lines. Excellent reading for seven-year-olds trying their wings, though the William Mayne title *A Small Pudding for Wee Gowrie*, with this author's unusual phrasing, should probably be reserved for reading aloud.

*Follow That Bus! Pat Hutchins, illus. Laurence Hutchins (The Bodley Head/Fontana Lions paperback)

Four Dolls Rumer Godden, illus. Pauline Baynes (Macmillan)
> The four stories which make up this handsome volume were originally published as separate, generously

illustrated books. If you were lucky enough to have known them in their original form, you may be saddened to see them now cheek-by-jowl, their individual, subtly different flavours mixed, however tastefully. But nothing can take the shine from the author's luminous prose, and the stories stand alone. Each involves real people, as well as a doll whose essential character shines through, despite Rumer Godden's adherence to her own rules: no movement, except through human agency, no chatty 'coming alive' as an easy way of relating. But the depth of *feeling* in these stories is intense. Pauline Baynes's black-and-white illustrations are expressive and appropriate, and her colour plates—two to each story—superb. The book is one to be treasured—and you may find one or more of the originals in the library, as a real treat.

Gobbolino, the Witch's Cat Ursula Moray Williams (Harrap/Puffin paperback)
A wonderfully satisfying read-aloud story about an engaging kitten, born into a witch's household, who longs to become part of an ordinary family. See also *Adventures of the Little Wooden Horse* (p. 121).

The Ha Ha Bonk Book Janet and Allan Ahlberg (Viking Kestrel/Puffin paperback)

Hans Andersen: His Classic Fairy Tales Erik Haugaard, illus. Michael Foreman (Gollancz/Gollancz paperback)

Invitation to a Mouse and other poems Eleanor Farjeon, illus. Antony Maitland (Pelham Books/Knight paperback)
Eleanor Farjeon was born over one hundred years ago, but her poetry speaks directly to that core in children which is enduring. Curiosity about the world and its ways, protest at the requirements of adults, concern for animals and wonder at nature and its miracles fill the

pages of this deftly arranged and sensitively illustrated collection of poems. A prior word from parent or teacher explaining that the world described has been left a whole century behind will open the way for children to reflect on the eternal nature of the concerns of young humankind—and enjoy the precision and flow of well-crafted verse. Finally 'Mrs Malone'—

> Whose havings were few
> And whose holding was small
> And whose heart was so big
> It had room for us all . . .

is seldom encountered these days, and is worth the price of the whole book, paperback *or* hardcover.

The Julian Stories Ann Cameron, illus. Ann Strugnell (Gollancz/Fontana Lions paperback)
There are six stories in this attractively produced book, and each strikes a singular note. This is not just another collection of simple 'at home' stories. To begin with, Dad features rather more strongly than Mum; and Dad has style, imagination and a natural flair for fun. In the first story, he is making a special pudding for the boys' mother, who is out shopping. While he is taking a nap, the boys try the tiniest taste . . . with predictable results. But there is nothing predictable about their father's response to this outrage! In another story Julian, who relates the stories, inadvisedly tells his little brother Huey that a catalogue is 'a big book full of pictures of hundreds and hundreds of cats. And when you open it up, all the cats jump out and start running around.' Their father's ingenuity is strained to the utmost to cope with Huey's disappointment when the catalogue arrives, but cope he does, with an originality born of long practice. These are good, well-rounded stories, beautifully illustrated in black-and-white by Ann Strugnell. But it

is the narrative itself which sets them apart. Ann
Cameron uses language assuredly to create characters
one can believe in. Her children are children, direct
and enterprising. Their conversation is credible, their
behaviour utterly believable but never stereotyped.

*The Juniper Tree and Other Tales from Grimm ed. Lore
Segal, illus. Maurice Sendak (The Bodley Head)

*Little Bear's Feather Evelyn Davies, illus. Jane Paton
(Hamish Hamilton)
Little Bear is a small Red Indian boy who aspires to
recognition by his tribe, and is successful in the end.
The black-and-white illustrations are plentiful and
explicit; people, birds and animals are sympathetically
drawn in a story which presents human values
thoughtfully. (*Run for Home*, by the same author and
artist, is worth watching for, too.)

The Magic Finger Roald Dahl, illus. Pat Marriott
(Allen & Unwin/Puffin paperback)
Mr Gregg and his two sons, William and Philip, love
to hunt and shoot—until the heroine of this fast-
moving story uses a particular capacity she possesses
for creating magic and mayhem and leaves them all
with wings instead of arms—even their mother, whom
one supposes must be seen as an accessory both before
and after the event. Well-told, beautifully rounded and
generously illustrated, this is a riotously successful book.

Nancy Nuttall and the Mongrel Catherine Cookson,
illus. Carolyn Dinan (Macdonald)
Picture book format, but of seven- to eight-year-old
interest. Nancy dreams of her own room, a desk, a
chair and a dog. But her mother is not enthusiastic.
The resolution is heart-warming, the illustrations
charming.

Nurse Matilda Christianna Brand, illus. Edward Ardizzone
(Hodder & Stoughton)

'Once upon a time there was a huge family of children,
and they were all terribly, terribly naughty.' How
could such a story fail? On the third page, a catalogue
of typical crimes seals the contract; adult reader and
child listener alike are snared, and held. There is an
air of wild farce about the Edwardian Browns. To
begin with, there are so many children that names are
seldom repeated. The effect is dazing. Their fond and
blinkered Mama leaves them to the servants, upon
whom unspeakable atrocities are perpetrated—until
the unlikely Nurse Matilda arrives. Author and artist
were cousins and first heard 'Nurse Matilda' stories
from their joint grandfather, many, many years ago.
Reflection suggests that children haven't, after all,
deteriorated, except, perhaps, in their capacity for
diabolical initiative. 'Miss Helen has poured syrup into
all the Wellington boots . . .' 'Little Quentin had
drawn flowers up all the walls and was watering them
from the big brown nursery teapot . . .' 'Sophie was
shampooing Henrietta's hair with glue . . .' For good
measure, several further titles keep up the standard,
the pace and the riotous tongue-in-cheek action.

*Oh How Silly! and **Oh That's Ridiculous!* ed. William
Cole, illus. Tomi Ungerer (Methuen/Magnet paperback)

Old Peter's Russian Tales Arthur Ransome,
illus. Faith Jaques (Cape/Puffin paperback)

Arthur Ransome is widely known as the author of the
Swallows and Amazons books, which, with their
holiday adventure themes, will be loved by many
children once true fluency is established in the 'next
stage up'. It is hardly surprising that Ransome's one
collection of fairy tales—reflecting his love, as a young
man, of the wide plains, swift rivers and great forests

of Russia—should be as readable today as then. His
capacity for storytelling is superb, his belief in their
worth intense. 'No people who really like fairy stories
ever grow up altogether,' he says in his 1915 preface.
These stories will help modern children to retain their
sense of wonder, and give them endless enjoyment.

*Peter Pan and Wendy May Byron, illus. Mabel Lucie
Attwell (Hodder & Stoughton)

The Pirate Ship and Other Stories Ruth Ainsworth,
illus. Shirley Hughes (Heinemann)
    A wonderful present for a five-to-eight family, this
    handsome hardcovered volume. Ruth Ainsworth is
    tested and proven as a storyteller for small children.
    There is neither dull moment nor discordant note in
    this flowing, engrossing collection, which, with Shirley
    Hughes's stylish pictures, will be treasured for years.

The Pocket Mouse Barbara Willard, illus. M. Harford-
Cross (Julia MacRae)
    A gentle story, sensitively related. Colin feels
    understandably nervous about being away from home
    for the first time, and takes his toy mouse in his pocket
    for company. From the pen of an author whose books
    for much older children have brought her fame, this is
    a nicely shaped story, beautifully told.

Poems for Seven-Year-Olds and Under Helen Nicoll (ed.),
illus. Michael Foreman (Viking Kestrel/Puffin paperback)
    A well-produced, sensitively chosen collection, this:
    good to handle and to use. The editor has selected her
    material from a wide and varied field and has arranged
    the poems in appropriate sections: 'Fur and Feather',
    'Family and Friends', 'Dinner Time', 'Sea and Shore'
    and so on. But why not *over* seven? Surely much of this
    poetry would speak directly to eights!

Puppy Summer Meindert Dejong, illus. Anita Lobel
(Lutterworth)

Two children staying with their grandparents for the
summer set off to bring home the puppy of their choice
from a neighbouring farm—and fetch up with three.
Grandma and Grandpa are just as soft-hearted as the
children, and an enchanted (if busy) summer is had by
all. This author has a wonderful feeling for animals *and*
for people, and the hazy warmth of summer pervades
the simply told, but memorable story. The black-and-
white illustrations reflect the gentle, engrossing nature
of each day, as lived by a pair of loving, old-style
grandparents and two eternal-style children.

*Rooms to Let Margaret Mahy, illus. Jenny Williams
(Dent)

Round the Christmas Tree ed. Sara and Stephen Corrin,
illus. Jill Bennett (Faber/Puffin paperback)

A varied collection of Christmas stories for 'under-
nines', which will give good service throughout this
whole period. Many excellent authors are represented,
Jill Bennett's illustrations are suitably exuberant for
the theme, and the dust-jacket is a festive treat in red
and green, complete with Father Christmas.

The Saga of Noggin the Nog Oliver Postgate, illus. Peter
Firmin (Kaye and Ward)

Ten small, slim, square volumes whose contents are as
pleasing as their covers. On the one hand, each is a
spoof on the Viking saga form; on the other, the tales
are inventive, vigorous, and amusing. Each begins on a
high note of mock dignity: 'In the Lands of the North,
where the black rocks stand guard against the cold sea,
in the dark night that is very long, the men of the
Northlands sit by their great log fires, and they tell a
tale. They tell of Noggin, Prince of the Nogs . . .'

The illustrations are robust and engaging, and reflect the buoyant action of the text exactly. I lament the passing of these delectable little books. You may find them still in libraries, with luck. (Note that *Three Tales of Noggin, Vols 1 and 2* are still in print. These are easy-reading 'Noggin' collections which are useful in their way, but not to be compared with the 'Saga'.)

The Squirrel Wife Philippa Pearce, illus. Derek Collard (Longman)

This must surely be one of the most moving and satisfying tales ever told. It is an original fairy story which, as a fairy tale should, holds reader or listener spellbound from first to last word. Philippa Pearce's limpid style is incomparable, the story itself—of Jack the swineherd, whose courage and kindness is rewarded by the gift of a squirrel-turned-woman as wife—memorable. The squirrel wife herself is no mere chattel; her caring and courage equal Jack's, and lead inevitably to a happy ending. The book itself is exquisitely produced, each page framed in a decorated border. A gem, if you can find it in library or secondhand book shop.

Stories for Seven-Year-Olds and *More Stories for Seven-Year-Olds* Sara and Stephen Corrin, illus. Shirley Hughes (Faber/Puffin paperback)

Thing Robin Klein, illus. Alison Lester (Oxford)

The theme of an oversized egg which hatches into a dinosaur—or a dragon, or another inappropriate creature—is not new. This fact has not prevented Robin Klein from bestowing freshness and credibility upon her version of the phenomenon. Thing is a baby stegosaurus who hatches from the rock which Emily has acquired as substitute for the pet she is forbidden (by crusty, resident landlady Mrs McIlvray) to keep.

Thing himself is engaging. When not romping with
Emily in flat or park—where he learns to 'freeze' on
command, thus passing as an ornamental fence, cactus,
or piece of sculpture—he watches television. Naturally,
he is discovered by Mrs McIlvray, and just as
naturally, he is saved from exile to a museum, at the
eleventh hour. Burglars arrive while all human
residents are absent, and Thing saves the day! The
factor which saves the story, in this welter of stereotype
and predictability, is the strength and clarity of Robin
Klein's prose. The colour and black-and-white
illustrations are both liberal and lively.

The Three Toymakers, Malkin's Mountain and *The Toymaker's
Daughter* all by Ursula Moray Williams,
illus. Shirley Hughes (Hamish Hamilton)
Sadly out of print, this is a memorable trilogy which
has the capacity to engross and enchant children of
seven and over. The three volumes tell the story of
Marta, a beautiful but unpleasant doll who is made by
Malkin, a powerful and mysterious toymaker, in an
attempt to win The King's Prize and defeat his rivals,
Peter Toymaker and young Rudi. The age-old theme
of the triumph of good over evil is used here to show
Marta's ultimate transformation, through the power of
love, to a real child. The story takes place in a folk-tale
land which is Scandinavian in essence.

A Time to Laugh: Funny Stories for Children ed. Sara and
Stephen Corrin, illus. Gerald Rose (Faber paperback)
A wide-ranging collection of stories, some funny, some
ridiculous and all entertaining. In common with the
other anthologies edited by this reliable pair, *A Time to
Laugh* can be safely recommended. In time, the tales
range from Aesop, through Andersen and Kipling to
A. A. Milne and Ruth Ainsworth. In quality, they are
uniformly suited to the taste of seven-year-olds—and

Gerald Rose's illustrations are appropriately jaunty.

Turkish Fairy Tales Eleanor Brockett, illus. Harry and
Ilse Toothill (Muller, Blond & White)

The Village Dinosaur Phyllis Arkle, illus. Eccles Williams
(Brockhampton Press/Puffin paperback)

Dinosaurs have universal appeal and do not date. This
one, known familiarly as 'Dino', becomes the special
charge of Jed Watkins, a small boy hitherto noted only
for his ordinariness. Utterly improbable events and a
predictable finale ensure enjoyment. This is rousing
stuff for newly-fluent seven-year-olds, or for easy
listening. The pictures are in keeping with the flavour.

Wildcat Wendy and the Peekaboo Kid Nancy Chambers,
illus. James Hodgson (Hamish Hamilton/Fontana Lions
paperback)

The sort of story which ought to be the start of a
series. Children ask for 'another book like *Wildcat
Wendy*' and one is obliged to inform them that there is
not another. In more ways than one, there is not!
Wildcat Wendy (she prefers just 'Wildcat') is on a
mission which must be completed before the moon is
full. She must deliver a message from Tiny John
Tripper to the Peekaboo Kid in the Canyon del Oro.
Ultimately, both she and the Kid (who proves to be an
ally) pit themselves against Hedlock Henry and his vile
gang, triumphantly thwarting their dastardly plans and
sending them packing (and yelping!). The adult reader
will relish the tongue-in-cheek Wild West dialogue,
which in no way undermines the honest action of the
story. Wildcat herself, and her story, have style.

You Can't Catch Me! Michael Rosen, illus. Quentin
Blake (Deutsch/Puffin paperback)

5

Eight-Year-Olds
and Their Books

Eight comes in with a roll of drums. The violins tail off, and the brass takes up the theme—heard earlier, around six, but stronger and more confident now. For the eight-year-old *is* capable!

Eight to twelve used to be that period of childhood which adults, looking back, remembered for its fun, its opportunities for co-operating with the kids next door in endless, complicated games involving huts, clubs and gangs, with anything and everything to hand put to some inventive use. Sadly, the boundaries of adolescence (a term quite unused forty years ago) have been pushed further and further into childhood, so that many eleven- and twelve-year-olds have thrown off the trappings of childhood and have cast themselves, with society's 'help', in a role which sits ill on their young shoulders.

This makes the years between eight and ten even more important than they used to be. Parents who will turn a blind eye on house and garden for these few short years, and find ways of providing the planks, ropes, boxes and general 'junk' which this age so loves (and which requires ingenuity, rather than expense, in its assembly) will discern the benefit in their children's developing initiative and energy.

And inside: this is the age for collecting stamps, postcards and containers, assembling models, carving and whittling wood, making books for use as scrapbooks and diaries, or for housing club rules, or original stories. Crossword puzzles in all their variations start to appeal to capable reading and writing eight-year-olds, with their wide range of spontaneous reference and their ability to handle a suitably clear dictionary. Scrabble and similar word games in small doses to begin with, and with uncritical adult help) are excellent evening and rainy day occupations, as are card games, Monopoly and other board games, paper-cutting and -folding, present-making, simple macramé, magic . . . the list is a long one.

Most eight-year-olds love to cook, too, and some of them want to sew. Others want to make large constructions—trolleys are popular—and need considerable parental help, if success is to crown their efforts. Building kites, improvising tents . . . eight-year-olds want to succeed, believe that they can, and deserve our help. Inevitably, their capacity often falls short of their ambition, for their power of self-assessment has developed considerably, and disillusionment can result. A kite that won't fly, a garment for bear or doll that falls apart at the seams, can induce a scene which takes everyone back a few years—and is all the more vehement because of the eight-year-old's tendency to self-dramatization.

This is the year which, I believe, confirms or denies the child's entry into the privileged company of 'real readers'. This does not mean that children who are not reading fluently as nine approaches have *no* chance of becoming committed readers, but it does mean that adults—particularly parents—should look honestly at the situation and look for ways of increasing enthusiasm for books and the ability to read.

You will note that I mention 'enthusiasm' before 'ability'. This is because enthusiasm is essential to the development of fluency. Only practice helps, at a certain stage of reading, and this stage is that point of achievement commonly known as a 'seven-year-old reading age'. Many children attain this level by seven—and have not moved on, by nine or ten. (We see many such children in our Reading Centre.)

What has happened to them? We are usually assured that they made a satisfactory start. Testing them reveals that most of the so-called 'skills' are intact. These children are equipped to become good readers, but they are not using the equipment. From the stage described above, there is only one way of becoming a fluent, responsive reader, a person whose eyes swing along the line and down the page while meaning pours into the mind. The magic formula? Practice! In my experience, the difference between a twelve-year-old who reads with effortless pleasure and one who limps painfully along is likely to be thousands of hours of practice, on the one hand, and virtually none, on the other.

What has motivated one of these children to give him- or herself this practice? Certainly not virtue, or a strong sense of duty. Children just aren't like that! No, fortunate children— the fluent readers—discover somewhere along the line that it is possible to disappear into a book and find themselves in a different place; that the good book is a 'slice of life', with all of life's potential for joy and pain, for fun, fear, wonder and all other human emotions, as well as countless experiences. Once started, these children are launched on to a happy cause-and-effect roundabout where enthusiasm leads to effort, effort leads to success, success leads to repeat perform- ance (practice!), increased fluency and greater enthusiasm.

Where must they get this practice? In their own homes. Allowing forty weeks of school attendance and twelve weeks of holidays per year, children spend more than three times as long awake *out* of school, as in. (This estimate assumes five hours per day in the schoolroom, six hours awake at home on schooldays, and thirteen hours per day awake at home during weekends and holidays.) Blaming schools, when children are seen to be 'non-' or 'retarded' readers does not seem very reasonable, in the face of these details. And there is another common stumbling-block. Some children arrive at a point where they have run out of resources; they can decode words and sentences, but their experience, vocabu- lary and understanding lags.

The remedy for both these ills—lack of enthusiasm, and lack of resources—is, of course, the subject of this book: the provision of the right sort of books, plus parental willingness to read aloud, with all the reorganization of lifestyle which this provision and practice may require.

Some children, of course, 'find' reading for themselves, and are fortunate enough to locate a good source of books, as well. (Heaven be praised for good and caring teachers and librarians!) But such children are, sadly, less likely to appear in our media-ridden society than they were fifty years ago. Lacking encouragement and example, children are unlikely to be snared by books; and their chances recede rapidly as the years advance, for the gap widens between children who *do* read and children who don't, in the next stage up from this one. Now is the time for action.

As an antidote to possible gloom, let us start on a cheerful note with Joan Aiken's heroine, Arabel, and her raven, Mortimer. Arabel's father Mr Jones, a taxi driver, encounters Mortimer late one night, unconscious on the road. Naturally he takes the ungainly bird home and attempts to revive him with hot, sweet tea. *Unnaturally*, Mortimer contrives to spend the night in the fridge and is discovered next morning by Arabel (with delight) and Mrs Jones (with shock and horror).

From this point, events quickly get out of hand. The situation is fraught with outrageous possibility, all of which, and more, is realized. Mortimer himself is demoniac. His vocabulary consists of the one word, 'Nevermore!', and this he croaks at moments appropriate and otherwise, and especially down the phone. Joan Aiken's brisk and straight-forward prose brings the books within access of the average eight-year-old reader, and within the understanding of children several years younger. Her capacity for creating real people is imperceptibly but certainly at work throughout. Kindly, practical Mr Jones, his understandably irked wife and Arabel, that child of calm resolution and inventive bent, all spring from the page as flesh and blood.

Mortimer himself, larger than life and totally out of control, is every child's other self. Domestic carnage seems to erupt wherever he sets foot (or claw). That there are four books about Arabel and the unrepentant Mortimer—*Tales of Arabel's Raven*, *Arabel and Mortimer*, *Mortimer's Cross*, and *Mortimer Says Nothing*—is everyone's good fortune, as is the original choice of Quentin Blake as illustrator. No other artist could have reflected the lunatic seriousness of it all as Blake has done.

Eight-year-olds will almost certainly encounter Enid Blyton's Famous Five and Secret Seven adventure stories and, with their passion for 'more of the same', plod (or race) through both series. No harm will be done, provided the sugary, stereotyped good child/bad child images have their antidotes from other sounder sources. They may not, of course, unless you take positive action; but this is simple, if you can lay hands on a copy of *Little House in the Big Woods* by Laura Ingalls Wilder.

This is the first of eight books about the Ingalls family, their life and fortunes in America, in the second half of the last century. Although the books are, in a general way, autobiographical, they are told in the third person by Laura herself. A television series based on the books has become famous throughout the world, although its content is so far removed from that of the books as to make recognition almost impossible. The film plots are superficial and sentimental in the extreme, but an interest in the books has been engendered, and one will not complain about that!

The first book describes how five-year-old Laura, her older sister Mary and baby Carrie live with their parents in the big woods of Wisconsin, in a little grey house made of logs. Details abound of a daily life which demands hard work, patience and endurance from child as well as adult; a life lived close to animals and the elements, a life in which almost all effort must be devoted to the pursuit of food, clothing and warmth. In the next book about the family, *Little House on the Prairie*, Pa, ever ambitious, takes his family by covered wagon to the West, encountering hardship and hazard of every kind on the way.

Meanwhile, in distant New York State, a small boy called Almanzo Wilder, whose life is to be linked with Laura's, is also growing up on a farm; and his joys and woes and everyday concerns are documented in *Farmer Boy*, the second book to be published. Almanzo's background is one of greater prosperity than Laura's, but home-made and home-grown is still the rule. Meanwhile, Laura, her older sister Mary and baby Carrie are blessed with parents who show steadfast good sense, humour and acceptance of childish ways and needs, and there is fun and laughter in their lives, as well as the bleak reality of near poverty.

In contrast to the trivial and contrived adventures of the Famous Five, these are honest stories: stories of real human beings, working to create a true home, wherever they settle. The themes of love, mutual support and the worthwhileness of hard work are not pushed; they are simply there. In my experience, children of a wide age-range, and both sexes, love the Little House books. The frontier society portrayed by the books requires physical as well as emotional resilience, and danger, whether from bears or blizzards, is always present. And Pa's capacity for storytelling is sheer bonus!

One of my families of grandchildren, comprising boys of eight and six and a girl of four, heard the stories read aloud, book by book, early this year. After a long weekend of constant read-aloud sessions, their father besought them all to leave weekday instalments until the evening, when he could join the group. In vain; the boys came in from school every afternoon demanding, 'more Little House!', and Dad was obliged to make do with their spirited retellings later.

Eight Children and a Truck is the first in a series by Anne-Cath Vestly, which has been translated from the Norwegian original. Less well-known than the Little House books, and certainly recording less momentous events, it generates nonetheless the same atmosphere of human caring and effort. The family, this time, consists of four girls and four boys. In the first book, they are all—Mary, Martin, Martha,

Mark, Mona, Milly, Maggie and Little Mat, as well as Mum and Dad—squeezed into two rooms in a city flat. By the second book, *Eight Children Move House*, they have moved to a sizeable house in a wood, outside the town. Grandma has been brought home in triumph from her Old Folks' Home, and Stovepipe the dog is filled with understandable delight at his changed circumstances.

The children are spirited and inventive, but prey to the usual apprehensions of childhood. Mark, on the first day at his new school, hides behind the rubbish bins in the mistaken but firm belief that no one wants to play with him. Grandma relishes her opportunity to make a real contribution when Mum sprains her ankle and Dad is away for several days, and the children in their turn support *her*. There is plenty of action, and the humour is warm-hearted. Three more titles provide more of the same, with original variations on the standard, wholesome themes; in short, a wealth of rewarding listening for children between seven and ten. (It is worth noting that the children in these stories range in age up to twelve, which brings the books within interest level of older, slower readers and listeners.)

Pippi Longstocking by the Swedish writer, Astrid Lindgren, appeals perennially to an age-group which is obliged to accept dependence, and yet longs for freedom. For Pippi is no ordinary child. She lives by herself in Vilekulla cottage, as she is orphaned, though she is personally certain that her father, supposedly lost at sea, is currently King of a Cannibal Island and will reappear to claim her. Possessed of astonishing strength—she can pick up a horse!—Pippi lives a life of total freedom, confounding two policemen, who are sent to take her into care, by leaving them stranded on a rooftop. Tommy and Annika, two conventionally brought-up neighbouring children, are her abject slaves, though Annika's astuteness saves her from complicity in Pippi's worst excesses.

First published in Sweden in 1945 and subsequently, with two further titles, translated into many different languages,

Pippi was originally viewed by some adults with doubt and misgiving. Children, by contrast, have always been unstinting in their support and appreciation. But Pippi is a real child, not merely a caricature. Her humanity shines through, despite her sweeping disrespect for adult expectations and institutions. All three Pippi books will delight the eight-year-old—and adult readers who are prepared to laugh a little at the hypocrisy and posturing of their own world will find much to amuse them.

The real-life vicissitudes of Laura and Mary, the lively everyday doings of Anne-Cath Vestly's 'Eight' and the larger-than-life exploits of the redoubtable Pippi are diverting in the extreme, but provide more than mere entertainment for the questing eight-year-old. Self-awareness is growing fast, but another sort of awareness is taking form, too—the beginnings of realization that human beings are dependent on one another for the real necessities of life: mutual love and support, the sharing of joy and sorrow and generous physical help in times of hardship.

Stories which present human beings as real people, prey to all the doubts and fears of ordinary human beings, along with humankind's capacity for love and laughter, nourish this dawning awareness of relationship. And such stories need not be sober, and certainly must not preach.

The Shrinking of Treehorn by Florence Parry Heide is a case in point. Treehorn is shrinking; there is no doubt about that. Attempts to invoke adult concern, or even recognition of the phenomenon, fail. In fact, blame rather than help is Treehorn's lot.

> 'If you're Treehorn, why are you so small?' asked the teacher.
>
> 'Because I'm shrinking,' said Treehorn. 'I'm getting smaller.'
>
> 'Well, I'll let it go for today,' said his teacher. 'But see that it's taken care of before tomorrow. We don't shrink in this class.'

The Shrinking of Treehorn makes one ashamed to be adult. Treehorn himself, in contrast to his detached and platitudinous elders, is both realistic and resourceful. And by the time the shrinking problem is over, astute.

This is a deliciously funny little book, in which Edward Gorey's elegantly eloquent black-and-white illustrations play a vital part. The whole is not only funny; it is a penetrating comment on adult insensitivity to children. One cannot be sure that the eight-year-old notices this, but experience reveals that the humour is relished, and the satire suspected, if only unconsciously.

The Best Christmas Pageant Ever by Barbara Robinson is, quite simply, unique. Once encountered, it will feature in any discriminating family's Christmas read-aloud programme as long as there is an ear to listen. I am at the moment reading it to two adjacent granddaughters, for the third Christmas in succession.

Our only problem is my inability to continue, from time to time. It is just not possible to refrain from the sort of laughter which wells up from inside and convulses the whole frame, in the course of reading this splendid book, either aloud or silently. And the end is just as likely to move both reader and listener to tears.

The Herdmans are described on the first page as 'the worst kids in the world'. Their catalogued crimes tend to support this assessment, and one expects trouble when, due to a misunderstanding, they attend Sunday School on the day the cast for the Christmas Pageant is being chosen, and (with Mafia-style efficiency) seize the leading roles. No one, inside the story or out, can foresee the developments from this point, and they are too good to divulge. Published in paperback as *The Worst Kids in the World* (an unnecessary alteration, I consider), this is a priceless story. Probably at its best with ten-to-twelve-year-olds, but accessible to eight-year-olds, it also makes a wonderful present for a deserving adult.

Roald Dahl has become famous as a children's author

over the last ten years, though his first book, *James and the Giant Peach*, was actually published in 1961. His second book, *Charlie and the Chocolate Factory*, became a bestseller. Each new title from Dahl's pen is now eagerly awaited by a public which knows and reveres his name. Only the perennial Dr Seuss and the ubiquitous Richard Scarry have ever achieved such widespread acclaim; only the controversial Enid Blyton has ever eclipsed it.

To what must one attribute such success? Is it true that Dahl's work appeals immediately to all children? There is, certainly, considerable evidence to support this claim; but so, too, must one note that many teachers who are unacquainted with a wide range of children's books of quality (and many are lamentably uninformed) request 'the latest Roald Dahl' at library or bookshop because they know his name, and believe that he is popular. This means that, in New Zealand schools, if in no other, children are certain to encounter his work. No such guarantee applies to any other author, it seems. In our bookshop, we often try to divert such requests. 'Have you read *Stig of the Dump*?' we ask with studied casualness. 'Why not leave them to read *The Twits* themselves, as Roald Dahl is so popular?' It works sometimes, but not often enough.

Dahl *succeeds* one suspects, regardless of teacher-skill in presentation. Why? To begin with, his work is almost always funny—and humour is the most immediately accessible of all literary ingredients. (This predilection for humour can be seen in poetry, too. Many teachers will not risk anything 'serious'.)

Secondly, Dahl's work has, I believe, great appeal for those children in our society who are over-trained, over-clean and over-organized: children who seem to be starved of the sort of earthy humour which is childhood's own. In a world of bossy, decision-making adults, Roald Dahl's stories are attractively subversive. Predictably, those children whose lives are less circumscribed, whose families are more relaxed about speech and behaviour in general, are somewhat less impressed. Dahl's 'coarseness' certainly falls with greatest impact on the ears of the over-refined.

The Magic Finger and *Fantastic Mr Fox*, as mentioned in the last booklist, will be enjoyed by this age-group, too. The others will certainly be discovered in due course, by any reading child. One title stands out: *The BFG* (Big Friendly Giant), its inevitable component of vulgarity notwithstanding, has a quality of warmth and good humour which, in the context of an entertaining, even wildly exciting story, turns it into a fine book.

The BFG's personal language is so idiosyncratic as to defy description. Sophie, the small girl whom he abducts, and who subsequently takes *him* over, is full of courage, sound sense and enterprise. Their encounter with the Queen (yes, *the* Queen) is delicious; all three emerge splendidly, with the Queen in undeniable control. Her Majesty's quick ring around the Heads of State, to verify Sophie's and the BFG's story that the other, wicked giants have been gulping down the citizens of their respective countries, dozens at a time, is masterly.

> 'I *knew* there was something like this going on, Your Majesty,' the Head of the Army said. 'For the last ten years we have been getting reports from nearly every country in the world about people disappearing mysteriously in the night. We had one only the other day from Panama . . .'
>
> 'For the hatty taste!' cried the BFG.
>
> 'And one from Wellington, in New Zealand,' said the Head of the Army.
>
> 'For the booty flavour!' cried the BFG.
>
> 'What *is* he talking about?' said the Head of the Air Force.
>
> 'Work it out for yourself,' the Queen said.

The hardcovered edition of this book is particularly well produced, with large, clear print and a most attractive dust-jacket; an especially pleasing present for a child whose enthusiasm for the written word may be sluggish. Quentin Blake's illustrations achieve perfect harmony with this particular story; but then Blake is a kind caricaturist. His work has a vitality which is always compassionate, never derisive. His pictured people have a commitment to their endeavours which is always entire and unsophisticated. Quentin Blake reflects the Big Friendly Giant as he is, innocent and steadfast, and plays his part in producing a lovable book.

I have listed the other Dahl titles which are suitable for five to eights in their appropriate lists. You may notice, though, that I have not included the enormously successful *Revolting Rhymes*. I have no hesitation in beseeching you not to use this title with your children, until they have had the wonder and enjoyment which is their due, from the good old tales which Dahl so freely satirizes. No one, of any age, can resist a hoot of laughter at Dahl's clever, if crude, parodies. That the passing enjoyment of their doggerel fun should be allowed to rob very young children of the experience of the real Cinderella, Snow White and the Seven Dwarfs, and Jack and the Beanstalk is, however, unthinkable. Try to leave *Revolting Rhymes* until ten or over. It can only gain in the waiting.

Meanwhile, *It's Too Frightening for Me* by Shirley Hughes is an excellent read-aloud choice for eight-year-olds—and pelts along at such a rate that the least likely child will be rendered agog. It is also warm-hearted and funny, with a lovely tongue-in-cheek 'wicked landlord' (or rather 'landlord-imposter') theme which gives full rein to everyone's outrage, and ultimate jubilation. The author's own illustrations, several per page, are as lively and expressive as ever.

I have just encountered *Chips and Jessie*, by the same author, and found it enchanting. *Chips and Jessie* is for all the world like a Christmas pudding, packed with fruit, nuts and cherries, not to mention juicy plums. Its pervasive flavour of warmth and humour is like brandy poured over and lit. The result is, predictably, delicious.

At the beginning Chips, egged on by his friend Jessie

('You said you wanted to do it!'), introduces the book to its readers. This is a nice touch for a book which is, actually, a dramatic performance as well as a collection of stories. It serves the purpose of presenting all the characters, before the action begins. In the early days of reading aloud, many children are defeated by the need to keep already introduced characters in mind while a succession of others appear. It is comforting to be told, on a page which also has a cheerful picture of Chips announcing and Jessie urging ('Do hurry up and get on with it!') that,

> People like my mum and Jessie's mum are in it, of course, and Grandpa. And then, when Fred Laski and Winston and Spud Ellis, Becky, Big Joan and Little Joan and all that lot found out about there being this book about us, they had to go and shove in somehow like they always do. And we had to have my cat, Albert, in, and Jessie's dog, Barkis, because they're very important and there's my baby sister, Gloria. We couldn't very well leave her out, worse luck.

There are, in the event, four stories and, appropriately, a 'Finale'. A variety of techniques is used throughout the book, ensuring the rapt interest of any child one can imagine, from total non-reader to the fluent and able. One astonishing double spread reveals four separate techniques, presented vertically. Across the bottom, the storyline proceeds, informing us that Chips and Jessie are sitting on the kitchen table at Chips's house while Jessie tells Chips about 'a very spooky film she had seen on TV. It was about a man who had been locked up in a terrible prison, on an island from which no one could escape, even though he had done nothing wrong . . .'

Directly above, one sees Jessie narrating and Chips listening. Above them, the actual exchange appears in balloon form, and, higher still, its imaginary nature indicated by 'cloud'-style brackets, pictures from the film, remembered by Jessie and imagined by Chips. For good measure, on the extreme right, sharp-eyed viewers can discern Chico the hamster, thought to be irretrievably lost, making his determined way down through the wall cavity, until he is finally revealed, chirpily peering through the hole he has gnawed behind the sink. (This story is called 'Anyone Here Seen Chico?')

The use of so many different ways of communicating both action and speech brings the book within the reach of any child, and makes it, actually, a fascinating encounter for any age-group. Chips and Jessie themselves are real; quite unlike one another, but recognizably 'eight-ish' with all that age-group's vigour and initiative, limitations and good humour. One can safely predict that this entertaining and heart-warming book will become famous; and one can easily imagine several more volumes in the cheerful saga.

If your eight-year-old son or daughter happens to be your oldest child, you are moving into exciting waters, for eight is well endowed with 'classics', those hard to define but easy to recognize stories which can be relied upon to appeal to almost all children. *Pippi Longstocking* and the Little House books certainly come into this category; and next on the list are *Stig of the Dump* and *Charlotte's Web*.

Stig is a Stone Age boy, whom Barney discovers living in a chalk pit. He is inventive, energetic and totally independent of adult organization; in short, a child's other self. Clive King develops the relationship between the two boys with skill. Originally strange to one another, they co-operate before long in the fascinating task of improving Stig's living conditions. Free reign is given to every child's love of hut-and den-building, and of contriving and making-do; and of the universal longing for a secret friend, inaccessible to all others and particularly to adults. Is Stig real, does Barney imagine him, or does the author intend the story to be experienced as fantasy? We don't know, and it doesn't matter. *Stig of the Dump* is a book for children to dream and grow on.

Charlotte's Web is a wonderful book with a quite unlikely theme: the establishment of sympathetic understanding between a spider and a pig. That Charlotte, the spider, succeeds in saving Wilbur, the pig, from the hatchet and the bacon factory is extraordinary enough. That she also manages to persuade Wilbur of the inevitability and rightness of her own death, and that the author, E. B. White, successfully includes his youthful audience in the acceptance of this and other philosophical propositions—all from the mouth of the perceptive and articulate Charlotte—is nothing short of astonishing. There is, however, nothing morbid about *Charlotte's Web*; in fact, it is a witty, essentially happy book, with a singular capacity to hold a child's attention. Garth Williams's illustrations contrive a hearty but sensitive commentary, which has become, in the more than thirty years of Charlotte's literary life, essential to the experience.

The Hundred and One Dalmatians by Dodie Smith is splendid read-aloud stuff, and should certainly be tapped during this year. For this is a truly thrilling story. Unlikely in the extreme, but equally believable, it tells of parent Dalmatians, Pongo and Missis, whose brood of fifteen puppies is abducted by a villainous woman called Cruella de Vil. It is their spotted coats which attract her; horror of horrors, she proposes to turn them into articles of human apparel! Funny and sad by turn, *The Hundred and One Dalmatians* is triumphant in its entirety—as, of course, are Pongo and Missis (ably assisted by a network of outraged and enterprising dog friends) in retrieving their offspring.

In his unusual, short novel for children, *The Iron Man*, Ted Hughes adds to the list of modern classics which are appropriate for eight-year-old listening, or reading. Children enjoy it for its action, which is engrossing, but its mystery and symbolism transform it into a modern fable, the property of all age-groups. The opening sets the scene for the terrifying, enigmatic story which unfolds.

The Iron Man came to the top of the cliff.
How far had he walked? Nobody knows. Where

had he come from? Nobody knows. How was he made? Nobody knows.

Taller than a house, the Iron Man stood at the top of the cliff, on the very brink, in the darkness.

Among the villagers who become involved, only one boy is perceptive enough to have any understanding of the Iron Man's needs, or potential. The significance of the giant-monster's appetite for metal, and its ultimate battle with a space creature whose intentions are similarly obscure, will be different for all readers. About the book's appeal and worth there can be no doubt. *The Iron Man* is a notable book, which is certain to endure.

Philippa Pearce is generally regarded as one of the finest living writers for children. Her book, *Tom's Midnight Garden*, which won the Carnegie Medal in 1958, has been described, I believe justly, as the most likely modern children's novel to achieve classic status in the long term. I would defer its introduction for several years still, meanwhile ensuring that eight-year-old listeners are exposed to the suspense—and wisdom—of *The Battle of Bubble and Squeak*. Philippa Pearce's real strength is the unique spareness of her prose. One is hardly conscious of reading at all; only of meaning emerging, of places and characters becoming known, of people interacting in the way they must, given their individual personalities, ambitions and situations. Her text, here as elsewhere, has a total lack of contrivance or pretentiousness. It is as nearly perfect as language in support of character, setting and action can be.

Bubble and Squeak are gerbils. They are acquired by the Sparrow family in the age-old way of pets and the children who covet them:

'A boy at school gave them to me. Jimmy Dean's cousin. He gave them to me with the cage . . .'

Thus, at three o'clock in the morning, Sid Sparrow reveals his deception to his outraged mother and rather more sympathetic stepfather, the noise of the two gerbils' scuffling having sparked off parental apprehension about burglars.

There is, of course, far more in this book than the bare bones of the boy-gets-pets, boy-loses-pets, mother-relents theme. There is much about Sid's relationship with his stepfather, Bill, about his mother's relationship with them all, and about Sid's sisters, Peggy and Amy. There is to be no solution which will be easy for everyone, but we all *know* another family of people, by the time this book is over.

Philippa Pearce makes no attempt to align her characters on opposite sides of the question and then invoke the reader's sympathy for the side of her choice. To extend the comparison with Blyton's work: the Famous Five, the Secret Seven and other Blyton characters (who are indistinguishable, except in terms of gross stereotype) are always right. Anyone who opposes them is 'mean' and 'nasty', and is suitably and mercilessly dealt with—to the great joy and satisfaction of the triumphant heroes and heroines.

Does this matter, if the children are *reading*, and enjoying the experience? Perhaps not; I have never felt that banning Blyton was a useful move, anyway. But where do children learn to look at people and situations in a way which is likely to lead them to understanding and compassionate, rather than rigid and judging ways? From their families first of all. But from the sum total of their experiences, surely, and their reading must be seen as part of that experience. Sid's, Peggy's and Amy's mum, with all her rejection of the gerbils, emerges from *The Battle of Bubble and Squeak* as a lovable person, tortured by her contradictory emotions. Even at eight years of age, one can start to see that we are all creatures of diverse and inconsistent passions.

What about the real classics? Is the eight-year-old ready for *Treasure Island*, *The Wind in the Willows* and *Black Beauty*? Or *Robin Hood*, *King Arthur* and *The Arabian Nights*? The very best, most prolific readers will be self-propelled and you may well find them reading *The Lord of the Rings*, if they happen to encounter it. The decision may seem to be out of your hands. The problem touched on in a previous chapter—that of the unusually able reader who is seen to be gulping down books which are certainly beyond his or her reach emotionally and intellectually—is one which may not excite sympathy in the breasts of those whose children need persuasion to read at all, but it is a pressing one nonetheless. The only solution— and it is not an easy one—is to cater so well for this voracious reader that there is always a range of suitable books on hand. This will mean determined tapping of the resources of school and public libraries, and making sure that home-owned books are enduring ones. For this child, more than any other, will probably be prepared to read and re-read.

One of my grandchildren comes into this category at the moment. His mother reports that the *Just So Stories*, *Alice in Wonderland*, *The Jungle Book*, all the Little House books, *Swallows and Amazons* and *Swallowdale*, as well as a wide selection of collected fairy stories (Lang's Colour Fairy Books and the many excellent retellings by Ruth Manning-Sanders), are all read time and time again—along with the irresistible adventures of that all-time comic-strip boy detective favourite, Tintin. In between, we work at finding additional titles—and are often surprised. For this sort of reader has, and will always have, I suspect, a taste which is wide-ranging, and often undiscriminating.

My grandson may be seen with his head in an adult textbook at one moment, and his attention utterly captured by a new picture book intended for his little sister the next. Nothing is ever described as either 'babyish' or 'too hard'. Books are books, in Anthony's calendar.

At the end of this chapter, I have included a list of classics which, in my experience, appeal to average eight-year-olds. Be certain, if you decide to try one of these with your child, that you read it yourself, ahead of time. Apart from all else, you will make a better job of the reading aloud if you are freshly familiar with the book's contents. And, as you are probably by now attuned to your own child's taste and depth of understanding, you will be better able to judge the book's chances of success. Dependence on your own childhood recollection of a story cannot compare with on-the-spot assessment.

Alice in Wonderland is, in my opinion, a book which the present generation of adults consistently misjudges. The real Alice was ten years old at the time of the boat trip on the river at Oxford, which began it all; that famous summer's day jaunt, during which the young don, Charles Dodgson, began to tell the story. Why then, should we expect five- and six-year-olds to understand and enjoy the inspired nonsense that is the essential Alice? Eight, on the other hand, has much to recommend it as an introductory point. We are told that the 'book' Alice has had 'seven-and-a-half years to learn rules and regulations' and to use reason. She does so unerringly, and this appeals to intelligent eights, especially as the outcome is almost always hilarious.

> 'Take some more tea,' the March Hare said to Alice, very earnestly.
> 'I've had nothing yet,' Alice replied in an offended tone, 'so I can't take more.'
> 'You mean you can't take *less*,' said the Hatter: 'it's very easy to take *more* than nothing.'

That Charles Dodgson alias Lewis Carroll had a good working knowledge of the ways of children—even little girls raised correctly in Victorian nurseries—is apparent in Alice's response to the Hatter's smartness on this occasion.

> 'Nobody asked *your* opinion,' said Alice

with more energy than refinement.

Alice herself is worthy of close examination, especially if you have only the haziest recollection of her character and conduct. I find it surprising that she has not been taken up by the extreme feminists; a more vigorous, less subservient female child could hardly be imagined.

Through all her adventures, from her first sight of the White Rabbit onwards, Alice behaves not only with courage, but with confidence and the expectation of fair treatment.

A succession of encounters with male animals—for whom Alice has little respect, as their remarks and behaviour invariably reveal them to be either confused or frightened, or both—serves only to emphasize Alice's good (female) sense, and robust spirit. The Duchess and the cook, as the first females encountered, reinforce one's suspicion that the author had slight belief, if any, in the frailty of the 'gentle' sex.

> 'Here! you may nurse it a bit, if you like!' the Duchess said to Alice, flinging the baby at her as she spoke. 'I must go and get ready to play croquet with the Queen,' and she hurried out of the room. The cook threw a frying-pan after her as she went out, but it just missed her.
>
> Alice caught the baby with some difficulty, as it was a queer-shaped little creature, and held out its arms and legs in all directions, 'just like a star-fish,' thought Alice. The poor little thing was snorting like a steam-engine . . .

Robust stuff, to say the least. Roald Dahl does not, after all, have the monopoly of vulgar verbal exchange and rough-and-tumble action.

There is a richness and virtuosity about Rudyard Kipling's *Just So Stories* which one cannot exactly replace from any other source. These tales were told, originally, to the author's eldest child, Josephine, and this 'meant-to-be-heard' quality rings through the book. The language may seem, to some modern readers, somewhat archaic and ornate. But it is memorable, and each story is so embellished with repetition, and so rhythmical, that children listen, entranced. One vital condition is that the adult must read with confidence, for these stories require performance. Once the style is established, the words roll off the tongue:

> In the High and Far-Off Times the Elephant, O Best
> Beloved, had no trunk. He had only a blackish,
> bulgy nose, as big as a boot . . .

The *Just So Stories* are full of resounding phrases, which,
with repetition, tend to pass into the family vernacular. In
the case of my own family, 'The great grey green greasy
Limpopo River, all set about with Fever Trees' (alias a
stream which made its sluggish way through a patch of
native bush at the bottom of the garden) featured in
innumerable games. And a six-year-old son, when my last
child was born, wrote me a marvellously mis-spelt letter
which finished: P.S. Have you forgotn the sispendas? (For
reference, see 'How the Whale Got his Throat'.)

About fairy and folk tales, I can only say that now you
should feel free to try the full range, without too much fear of
nightmares or other upsets. Ruth Manning-Sanders is a
name to watch for. Her collections, entitled severally *A Book
of Dragons*, *A Book of Witches*, *A Book of Princes and Princesses*,
and so on, have remained in print, with regular additions
and reprints, for over twenty years; a distinction which, in
these days of publishing cut-backs, can only mean that the
books continue to sell. All are certainly available from
libraries and some are for sale in paperback form. But a
hardcovered copy of your own or the child's choice as a
birthday or Christmas present will be cherished. Each
volume is superbly produced, with the delicate, detailed and
yet spirited illustrations of Robin Jacques faithfully reflecting the mood of the collection.

Tolkien's *The Hobbit* will be a great joy to the good reader,
as nine approaches, and will be listened to with pleasure by
most children in this age bracket. Bilbo Baggins is a home-
loving rather than venturesome hobbit; and hobbits are '. . .
a little people, about half our height, and smaller than the
bearded dwarves . . .' Bilbo is persuaded against his will to
undertake a campaign to search out and kill the dragon
Smaug. He is a reluctant, even unlikely, hero, but his

perseverance and quality of steadfast courage lead to success. Tolkien's language, while complex in parts, has a
colloquial ring to it which matches the earthiness of the plot.
Those children who love *The Hobbit* will read it time and
again, for it has an epic quality which must be experienced to
be understood. And they are assured of more to come, for the
substantial trilogy *The Lord of the Rings*, while not a sequel to
The Hobbit, nonetheless relates to it at a crucial point. (*The
Lord of the Rings* was written ostensibly for adults, but
advanced readers of eleven and over often take it as their
own, and thrive on it.)

This is a crucial year for poetry, which must continue to
have a place in a child's listening, if it is to endure as a form at
all. All too often, poetry slips away and thereafter drifts
about in a sort of literary limbo, to be greeted with indif-
ference and embarrassment, if not outright dislike, when the
requirements of 'outside' examinations necessitate its
revival at secondary school.

Eight-year-olds are sensitive and responsive, and have not
yet become prey to the self-consciousness which our society
commonly provokes in children who are approaching
puberty. In my experience they listen with interest and
enjoyment to poems on a wide range of themes, and of widely
differing types. *I Like This Poem*, an original Puffin collection
for which each poem was submitted by a child, with reasons
for its choice, offers an opportunity to discuss this choice
without any artificiality. As in all anthologies, one will not
use all the poems. There is no field in which personal taste is
more likely to differ than this. Lucky the child who
encounters a teacher somewhere along the line who loves
poetry and communicates this love! Luckier still the youngster who listens to poetry read aloud at home, as part of
everyday life. The collections mentioned in earlier chapters
and lists will provide good starting-points for selection.
Several more have been included in the eight-year-old list.

One could write a whole volume about the fields opening
up to the really fluent and committed reader, as nine

approaches. Fortunately, this next-up group is better catered for in both reviewing magazines, articles and books, than the one under discussion here. But direction from interested adults is still essential, if such children are not to grow through this stage without tapping the vast and wonderful resources which are available for their special reading pleasure.

I have found, for example, that the modern passion for science fiction, or anything concerning space, is inclined to crowd an interest in history out of children's lives. Surely, the ways in which people have lived in times past must have potential satisfaction for children with alert and questioning minds? And the best historical fiction is so exciting! A child reader can feel, with justification, that 'I could have done that!' as the necessities of life are gleaned from a stubborn world by ingenuity, dexterity and hard work, battles fought and won, as tragically as ever, but perhaps more honestly, hand to hand. In a certain type of modern space fiction, all issues are resolved by the ultimate pressing of buttons. Shabby stuff which insults a child's intelligence.

Cynthia Harnett's books, incorporating as they do this fine author's own meticulous black-and-white illustrations, make absorbing reading for the able nearly-nine-year-old, and provide a wealth of fascinating detail about things and methods, as well as people. *The Wool-Pack*, which won the Carnegie Medal over thirty years ago, is an utterly absorbing tale set in the Cotswolds in the fifteenth century; while my favourite, *The Load of Unicorn*, involves the first English printer William Caxton. More particularly, from the child's point of view, it documents the doings of Bendy, the apprentice, in fifteenth-century London, implicated against his will in a plot to keep a load of paper ('Unicorn' by brand) from his master. High intrigue, certainly; but the ordinary, everyday fun of being a child, in any century, is there too, with a story which impels attention to the last page.

Rosemary Sutcliff is an author whom many children will grow to love in years to come. Meanwhile, several of her

early books are worth seeking out. *The Armourer's House*,
Brother Dusty-Feet and *The Queen Elizabeth Story*, all 'light-
weight' as compared with her later works, nonetheless show
the true feeling for time and character which is this author's
hallmark. The first two of these are available currently, and
the third, in all probability, still owned by some libraries. I
am convinced that an attempt should be made to interest
children in the history of their own, and other races' development from earliest times. I am just as sure that for many
modern children no such effort is made.

Eight, rising nine, is a time of intense growth and expan-
sion. Children, in their imaginative lives, need the richness
and wonder which books have to offer, if their spirits are to
be nourished, their minds equipped to face the realities of the
world as they will inevitably experience them. For life is both
better and worse than we let them know in the early days. To
be equipped to reach out and seize its joys as well as to
confront and cope with its contradictions, children must
grow to be strong, flexible, able to love and to laugh. Good
books will help them to do these things.

A WORD ABOUT '-ISMS'

These days there is much discussion on the need to preserve
the young from exposure to racism, sexism and other
undesirable influences. Many people feel that children's
books should be ruthlessly combed for all such emphases,
and these removed entirely.

To what extent should we be concerned about such views?
To begin with, it has always been clear that those people who
are most vociferous in this cause are seldom themselves
informed about literature in general, or children's books in
particular. Certainly, the 'cheaper' mass-market series are
often steeped in sexism, racism, snobbery and prejudice of
all kinds. (Refer to Biggles, the Famous Five and the Hardy
Boys, for example.) But is this true of the books of more
literary quality, commonly produced by reputable pub-

lishers? And is it desirable to submit books to any rigid censorship, banishing some and embracing others on such a narrow test?

The very best fiction mirrors the society from which it springs. Our best efforts should be reserved for the task of changing those things in our society which are cruel and unjust. Pretending that they do not exist—or never existed—is distortion, and cannot be expected to help any cause.

One of the most important functions of fiction is to encourage thinking: about good and bad ways of behaving, about cause and effect in human conduct, about the differences in people, their capacities and their needs. The thoughtful reformers, in any age and society, are the thinkers, and these are inclined to be, also, the readers. To imagine that a simple formula (show all the men in the book washing floors and all the women mending cars) will effect any substantial change in attitude is a delusion. The roles of men and women are changing, I believe, and children's books will naturally reflect these changes. But a 'put-up job' inevitably strikes a sour note. As a woman, I know that my best hope of convincing children that women have more than one role in life, is to demonstrate my capacity to pursue the role of my choice.

I feel strongly, however, that it is pernicious propaganda which tells children of both sexes that housekeeping and child-raising are demeaning occupations, when those of us who have engaged in them know that, like most jobs, they are only boring if poorly done, and that the best way to achieve satisfaction is to throw oneself into the job, whatever it is, and make of it an art. That men as well as women should be encouraged to make housekeeping a profession goes without saying. I believe that many more will, as society's expectations change.

I must voice my disapproval of one aspect of so-called 'non-sexist' books. Surely there is little point in trying to persuade girl readers, by example, to be physically violent—

presumably on the grounds that 'if aggression is good enough for boys, it's good enough for girls'? That there are already too many violent people in the world is apparent to all. Does it not make better sense to encourage gentleness in relationships, for both sexes? Women have traditionally been modifiers, rather than exponents of violence. Where will the world be if they abandon this role? There is little evidence of men's willingness to take it over.

I believe that small boys are rather ill served in our society and that this is a strong factor in the tendency of many of them to develop aggressiveness. From the beginning, male children are frailer than female; more male foetuses abort spontaneously than female, and male babies are less resistant to infection than female. Over all, two-year-old girls are likely to be superior to boys: better talkers, more agile, even more reliably potty-trained, and certainly more outgoing.

As early as two years of age, however, many boys are starting to be the subject of parental aspirations. They are expected not to cry as readily as girls, to 'stand up for themselves' and to be less dependent on human cuddling or comfort when hurt or frightened. By four, the differences are even more marked, with many more girls engaging in the sort of quiet pursuits which are likely to involve communication with other children and adults, as well as the increasing use of pencils, crayons and all the paraphernalia of writing and drawing, and, of course, reading. For many small boys, the printed word is already seen as 'unmanly'. They have, for better or worse, cast themselves in a 'physical' role.

At school, boys outnumber girls heavily as 'problem readers'. From discussions with parents over the years, I have gleaned the fact that almost all expect boys to be less book-ish, more active and more aggressive than girls. Is this expectation communicated to boys at an early stage, so that, finding themselves rather left behind in the things schools require of them by girls of their own age, they accept the evidence and unconsciously apply themselves to the business of helping to fulfil society's prophecies? Certainly, in those families where one finds more even treatment of small children, regardless of sex, one does find fewer submissive girls, fewer aggressive boys.

It is easy to blame fathers for the sex-casting which produces aggressive sons. In my experience mothers have a lot to do with it! In our bookshop, it is easy to persuade the mother of any two-year-old child, boy or girl, that one of the Thomas books by Gunilla Wolde will entertain and extend her child. But the companion Emma books? 'Oh, but it's for a *boy*,' is a common protest; and not merely from elderly aunts and grandmothers! Equally, it is often difficult to persuade women buyers that boys will relish Astrid Lindgren's *Pippi Longstocking* or one of Joan Aiken's Arabel titles—whereas *Stig of the Dump* or *Winnie-the-Pooh* are confidently and sensibly acquired for female children, despite the preponderance of male characters in both.

About the evils of racism, one can only tell children that the light-skinned races of the world have had, and in many places still have, much to answer for. Obviously, all right-minded parents will try, by example and education, to lead their children towards attitudes which are liberal and supportive, rather than rigid and restrictive. But once again, the artificial presentation of characters and situations intended to hammer home particular points of view is unlikely to help. Clinging to the view that anyone, child or adult, should be forced to adopt a particular view is, after all, bigotry, just as it was in the Middle Ages, or the eighteenth century. And children are not easily hoodwinked. Better, surely, to stick to honest representation, and permit and encourage open and thoughtful discussion.

It is my experience that children's racial, sexual and social attitudes depend far more strongly on the beliefs and behaviour of their parents, than on any 'teaching' they may receive, either at home or elsewhere. This is truly a field in which 'more is caught than taught'. With this in mind, we can surely avoid the worst excesses of censorship.

Book List 4

Books to Use with Eight-year-olds

All Sorts of Poems ed. Ann Thwaite (Methuen paperback)
A wide range of poems, all from the pen of living
authors. A useful and attractive collection for family or
school use.

Angry River Ruskin Bond, illus. Trevor Stubley
(Hamish Hamilton)
This is an unusually sensitive and honest story by an
Indian novelist of note. While serious in its tone, it is
within the reach of the average eight-year-old reader.
As an insight into the way some children in the world
live, and the responsibility they must take for their
own lives, this is a valuable book. This would not be
enough, of course; it is exciting, too.

Arabel and Mortimer, *Mortimer's Cross*, *Mortimer Says
Nothing* and *Tales of Arabel's Raven* all by Joan Aiken,
illus. Quentin Blake (Cape)

Aristide Robert Tibber, illus. Quentin Blake
(Hutchinson/Armada Lions paperback)
There is true treasure in this fast-moving tale of an
over-protected French boy who inadvertently drifts
across the English channel on an inflated mattress, and
becomes involved in a war game being played by
English children on the south coast. Wonderful
listening for any age.

The Armourer's House Rosemary Sutcliff,
illus. C. Walter Hodges (Oxford/Methuen paperback)

**The Battle of Bubble and Squeak* Philippa Pearce,
illus. Alan Baker (Deutsch/Puffin paperback)

A Bear Called Paddington Michael Bond, illus. Peggy
Fortnum (Collins/Fontana Lions paperback)
Named after the railway station on which he was
found, Paddington joins the Brown family—or rather,
takes over their lives. His capacity for creating chaos
out of order is impressive. The text is rather
sophisticated, but very funny, and the illustrations
evocative of an adored bear in the bosom of a loving (if
frequently distraught) family whose resilience amazes.
Numerous titles.

Beaver Towers Nigel Hinton, illus. Peter Rush (Abelard-
Schuman/Knight paperback)
This is an utterly engrossing, grab-you-on-the-first-
page story which I highly recommend for reading
aloud—especially to children who may be cynical
about the appeal of stories as against television
viewing. Philip ignores his parents' warning about
playing with his new kite on his own. 'It's big enough
to blow you away,' his mother said . . . Of course, it
does; but there the predictable ends, and a series of
hair-raising events begins. There is humour, warmth
and shared danger. Philip behaves with courage, and
makes true friends, whom he is obliged to leave behind
on his return home. Sequel: *The Witch's Revenge*.

Bellabelinda and the No-Good Angel Ursula Moray Williams,
illus. Glenys Ambrus (Chatto & Windus)
A modern story in an established tradition, by an
author who has been tested and proven over many
years. Bellabelinda, herself possessed of Powers (which
she has inherited from her great-great-grandmother,
who was a witch), rescues a small, lost, winged girl
who explains that she is a failed guardian angel and

longs to be installed in a happy family. This is achieved in the end, but not before Bellabelinda (a 'lollipop' lady by day and a babysitter by night) has almost come to regret her kind impulse in adopting 'Flipsy'. She and the Fogglebatch boys prove to be a lively combination! The incidents make good reading-aloud, and the whole is well-knit, and efficiently related; the work of an experienced craftsman. Glenys Ambrus's black-and-white illustrations, many of them whole-page, occur at almost every opening, and are nicely attuned to the flavour: energetically humorous, with natural warmth and vitality.

The Best Christmas Pageant Ever Barbara Robinson, illus. Judith Gwyn Brown (Faber) pub. in paperback under the title *The Worst Kids in the World* (Beaver Books)

The BFG Roald Dahl, illus. Quentin Blake (Cape/Puffin paperback)

A Book of Dragons, *A Book of Princes and Princesses* and *A Book of Witches* all by Ruth Manning-Sanders, illus. Robin Jacques (Methuen/Methuen paperback)

The Boy Who Sprouted Antlers John Yeoman, illus. Quentin Blake (Fontana Lions paperback)
    Billy Dexter's teacher had no idea what she was starting when she told him that 'As long as you set your mind on it and try hard enough, there's nothing you can't do.' How could she know that Billy would accept his friend Melanie's challenge to set about growing antlers? A highly individual theme, handled with verve and illustrated with Blake's usual brilliance. The result: a delectable book.

Bridget and William Jane Gardam, illus. Janet Rawlins (Julia MacRae/Puffin paperback)
    This author's capacity for breathing life into the

characters in her novels for adolescents obviously carries over into stories for a younger audience. Adult readers, along with eight-year-olds, will believe in Bridget, her family and the neighbours who become involved. Rare skill indeed. Reading such a superb mini novel could mark the beginning of real literary response.

*Brother Dusty-Feet Rosemary Sutcliff,
illus. C. Walter Hodges (Oxford)

*Charlie and the Chocolate Factory Roald Dahl,
illus. Faith Jaques (Allen & Unwin/Puffin paperback)

*Charlotte's Web E. B. White, illus. Garth Williams
(Hamish Hamilton/Puffin paperback)

*Chips and Jessie Shirley Hughes (The Bodley Head/
Fontana Lions paperback)

Christabel Alison Morgan, illus. Mariella Jennings
(Julia MacRae)
Bethan, the heroine of this engrossing short novel (one of the excellent Blackbirds), has twin sisters, two years older than she is and inherits two of everything (half worn out!). The family goat is thought to be having twins—'one for each of us,' say Julie and Jennifer. 'Do goats ever have threes?' asks Bethan. Christabel, the goat, goes on munching . . . Warm family background, with all the feeling and detail of farm life which marks this author's work. Attractive black-and-white illustrations.

C. L. U. T. Z. Marilyn Wilkes, illus. Larry Ross
(Gollancz/Piccolo paperback)
There is so much serious—even gloomy—science fiction inside covers that it is a joy to find a cheerful, rollicking spoof in which an outmoded robot becomes

part of a space-age family and sets about wrecking its serenity. (Shades of Amelia Bedelia, page 82!) The pictures are as lively as the text.

Conrad, the Factory Made Boy Christine Nostlinger (Beaver paperback)
Mrs Bartolotti did not mean to order a boy, but one arrived anyway, impressively packaged. She is loving, if rather dotty, and Conrad himself a delight. Mrs Bartolotti's efforts to keep Conrad (successful, in the end) make for a good rousing yarn while it's all underway.

Dinner at Alberta's Russell Hoban, illus. James Marshall (Cape/Puffin paperback)
This book is a joy to the whole world, not merely to eight-year-olds. In fact, one suspects that Arthur, his sister Emma, Emma's friend Alberta and Alberta's brother Sidney are actually all aged thirteen or fourteen (in strictly human terms). How can one tell, with crocodiles? Any parent who has managed to shepherd even one son to early manhood will recognize Arthur. How does Russell Hoban *manage*, with crocodiles (!) and an easy reading format? The illustrations are good, but the story could stand alone. I would buy an extra copy as an emergency gift for an adult friend who happens to have a sound sense of humour and is in need of a boost.

Eight Children and a Truck and *Eight Children Move House* Anne-Cath Vestly, illus. John Dyke (Methuen)

Fairy Tales Alison Uttley, chosen by Kathleen Lines, illus. Ann Strugnell (Puffin paperback)
From Spring to Spring: Stories of the Four Seasons Alison Uttley, chosen by Kathleen Lines, illus. Shirley Hughes (Faber/Faber paperback)

Alison Uttley's work spans fifty years, and is likely to endure for many, many more. Brought up in the country, she peoples her stories as easily with country lasses and stalwart farmers as with princesses and princes, and writes with true feeling for animals, fields and woods. For both these collections, Kathleen Lines has chosen stories which sit happily together. In each case the illustrations reflect the nature of the anthology and help to produce fine books; different, but equally satisfying.

Falter Tom and the Water Boy Maurice Duggan (Puffin paperback—Australia only)
This fantasy is told in simple, almost faultless prose. The story concerns an old, tale-spinning sailor whose nickname derives from his stiff leg, which gives him a faltering gait. His meeting with the water boy, his introduction to the green world of the under-sea and ultimate anguish of choice—between the real world and the ghostly world of the sea—together produce suspense and drama of a high order in a book of only sixty-four pages. A wonderful read-aloud treat.

*Fantastic Mr Fox Roald Dahl, illus. Jill Bennett (Allen & Unwin/Puffin paperback) (See Book List 3)

*Farmer Boy Laura Ingalls Wilder, illus. Garth Williams (Lutterworth/Puffin paperback)

The Ghost and Bertie Boggin Catherine Sefton, illus. Jill Bennett (Faber/Puffin paperback)
Bertie is the youngest of the Boggin family, and the subject of some victimization. He is especially pleased, therefore, to make the acquaintance of a genial ghost in the coal shed, and even more pleased when the ghost becomes his everyday friend. Nobody believes him, of course, but the evidence mounts . . .

A thoroughly enjoyable story, full of cheerful incident.
The occasional illustrations are delightful.

Grimble and *Grimble at Christmas* Clement Freud,
illus. Quentin Blake (Puffin paperback)
Two riotous, rather sophisticated stories which satirize
over-modern parents and their independent offspring.
The humour is for adults as well as worldly eight-year-
olds, but none the worse for that. Quentin Blake is just
right as artist.

Grimms' Fairy Tales Peter Carter (translator),
illus. Peter Richardson (Oxford)
A fine collection, translated with integrity. One senses
a feeling for the original, in Carter's preservation of the
sly humour and faintly camouflaged morals. The
illustrations add interest, colour and dignity.

Grump and the Hairy Mammoth Derek Sampson,
illus. Simon Stern (Methuen/Methuen paperback)
Prehistoric life has instant appeal for the young, and
Grump is a likeable if lugubrious example of cave-
dwelling humankind. His running battle with Herman,
the hairy mammoth, is amusing rather than scary, and
a tiger in need of help turns into a friend. Eight-year-
old humour abounds—'Soon he would be a tea-time
snack for a hungry tiger.' Agreeable line drawings
catch humans and animals at their least dignified and
most enjoyable.

The Hobbit J.R.R. Tolkien (Allen & Unwin/Allen &
Unwin paperback)

The Hundred and One Dalmatians Dodie Smith
(Heinemann/Piccolo paperback)

I Like This Poem ed. Kaye Webb, illus. Antony Maitland
(Viking Kestrel/Puffin paperback)

*The Iron Man Ted Hughes, illus. Andrew Davidson
(Faber/Faber paperback)

It's Funny When You Look at It Colin West (Century
Hutchinson)
> Some of these demented verses will defeat eight-year-
> old understanding, but then they may well bamboozle
> thirty-eight-year-old parents, so who cares? Shades of
> Ogden Nash, Hilaire Belloc and the funny moderns—
> and lashings of hitherto inexperienced dottiness which
> must be original West. More grease to his elbow. (He
> can even draw.)

**It's Too Frightening for Me* Shirley Hughes (Hodder &
Stoughton/Puffin paperback)

**James and the Giant Peach* Roald Dahl, illus. Nancy
Ekholm Burkert (Allen & Unwin/Puffin paperback)

Janni's Stork Rosemary Harris, illus. Juan Wijngaard
(Blackie)
> The illustrations in this picture-book sized, short novel,
> have a rare beauty. One senses painstaking research
> behind the delicate detail of period clothing, house
> exterior, and town and canal scene. No opening is
> without a picture—or two, or three—and each
> demands perusal. The story concerns Janni, who must
> sell his crotchety old grandmother's gingerbread, if the
> two of them are not to starve; Griet and her mother in
> their fine house in the next village—and Janni's
> longing for a stork to rest on his house roof, and bring
> luck to those within. A satisfying, beautiful book.

Jeffy, the Burglar's Cat Ursula Moray Williams,
illus. David McKee (Andersen Press/Puffin paperback)
> 'Nobody, seeing Miss Amity and her little cat walking
> down the street to the library on a Saturday morning,
> would have believed that Miss Amity was a burglar.'

This book has real virtuosity. The author's capacity for telling a good story in a totally engrossing way is put to the service of a tale which is improbable, hilarious, moving and, in the end, triumphantly resolved. The pictures are in the right mood.

The Light in the Attic and *Where the Sidewalk Ends* both by Shel Silverstein (Cape)

Captivating poems from an author whose work has become famous in America, and has at last been published in England. The sensitive and profound is all mixed up with the subversive and the hilarious in both these titles, which are, as a bonus, beautifully produced; large and sturdy, with the poet's own black-and-white drawings, which seem to have been accomplished in the same breath as the poetry. Wonderful presents for families of all ages and persuasions.

The Little Bookroom Eleanor Farjeon, illus. Edward Ardizzone (Oxford)

This is Eleanor Farjeon's personal collection from her many short stories; 'Chosen by herself', the title-page tells us. The book takes its title from a room in the author's childhood home; and Edward Ardizzone's illustration of the imagined small girl, immersed in a book and surrounded by toppling piles and crammed shelves of books, must be one of that famous artist's very best. Would that every child could have its own 'little bookroom'. 'No wonder that many years later, when I came to write books myself they were a muddle of fiction and fact and fantasy and truth . . .' this loved author tells us. Everyone will have his or her own favourite story. Mine is 'The Seventh Princess'.

Little House in the Big Woods and *Little House on the Prairie* Laura Ingalls Wilder, illus. Garth Williams (Methuen/Puffin paperback)

**The Load of Unicorn* Cynthia Harnett (Methuen)

**The Lord of the Rings* J.R.R. Tolkien (Allen & Unwin/
Allen & Unwin paperback)

The Magic Doll and Other Stories ed. Naomi Lewis,
illus. Harold Jones (Methuen paperback)
    A selection of outstanding tales, some old and none
    brand new, introduced by a master of her craft. These
    are all memorable stories which should not be lost.
    Their assembly here, with Harold Jones's superbly
    appropriate illustrations seems to guarantee their
    survival.

*The Magic Finger Roald Dahl, illus. Pat Marriott
(Allen & Unwin/Puffin paperback) (See Book List 3)

Marooned! Joyce Stranger, illus. Peter Rush
(Kaye & Ward)
    This realistic story presents a truly dangerous
    situation, and a small boy's reaction to it. Joyce
    Stranger is noted for her unsentimental and yet
    sympathetic portrayal of animals, which here adds
    honesty and conviction to a believable tale. Ably
    illustrated in black-and-white.

Midnight Pirate Diana Hendry, illus. Janet Duchesne
(Julia MacRae)
    An example of the well-produced Redwing Books,
    which are designed to follow this publisher's Blackbird
    series for five- and six-year-olds. Ida, who might be any
    age between seven and ten, has been sent, from her
    home by the sea, to stay with elderly aunts who divide
    their time between sleeping and issuing cautionary
    advice. Their dog Cleo is fat, bad-tempered and over-
    indulged. But the kitten who forces entry is utterly
    enchanting, if only to Ida, and all is well in the end.

Moffatt's Road Rachel Anderson, illus. Pat Marriott (Cape)

This wonderfully stout, utterly generous-looking book seems to have sprung from another age. Its story, too, refuses to concern itself with the possible—even likely—apprehensions of two well-brought-up English children who find themselves virtually abandoned in North Africa, when their plane makes an emergency landing in the middle of the Sahara desert and their mother is rendered incapable after a bump on the head. Instead, Louise and her younger brother Dickie are stout-hearted and realistic in the best tradition of British children Abroad in the nineteen-twenties. Fred, their baby brother, originally clean-smelling and freshly laundered, becomes 'grubby and sticky and damp', but also 'more of a person', Louise reflects. (He is ultimately naked, brown and very happy.) The reunion scene when they really *do* find their father 'Mr Moffatt, The Road Builder' will have the most blasé reader laughing and crying at the same time. A satisfying book.

The Old Nurse's Stocking Basket Eleanor Farjeon, illus. Edward Ardizzone (Oxford/Puffin paperback)

An intriguing setting for storytelling: an old nurse tells her charges a nightly tale which varies in length according to the size of the hole or ladder she is darning in one of their stockings. The stories vary in theme and setting but are uniformly fascinating—'The Sea Baby' must be one of the most enchanting stories ever told. An old collection this, which has more to offer than most of its modern counterparts. (Try the library for its out-of-print counterpart, *Jim at the Corner*, by the same incomparable author–artist combination.)

The Perfect Hamburger Alexander McCall Smith, illus. Laszlo Acs (Hamish Hamilton/Puffin paperback)

This story makes compulsive reading, which must be attributed in major part to the storytelling power of its author, for it positively surges along. Simple enough for an eight-year-old reader, compelling enough to guarantee adult attention to the last page, its unlikely theme—the pursuit of an elusive spice for a hamburger which will ensure old Mr Borthwick's continued livelihood as proprietor of an outmoded 'hamburger place'—is, in the event, gripping. The illustrations are good, but almost unnecessary. Who needs pictures, with a yarn of this quality?

The Phantom Fisherboy Ruth Ainsworth,
illus. Shirley Hughes (Deutsch)
Eights are only just ready for ghosts, and these are the gentle kind which amuse and puzzle rather than frighten. Wonderful read-aloud tales, imaginative and assured, with illustrations to match.

Pippi Goes Aboard, Pippi in the South Seas and *Pippi Longstocking* all by Astrid Lindgren, illus. Richard Kennedy (Oxford/Puffin paperback)

Please, Mrs Butler Allan Ahlberg, illus. Fritz Wegner (Viking Kestrel/Puffin paperback)
The humour in this delectable collection of observations on human existence in general and school life in particular is probably nine-to-elevenish, but I'd acquire a copy now, just in case it goes out of print. The action is accessible to eight-year-olds, the reading level is within reach and the liberally-sprinkled black-and-white pictures a joy.

Poems for Nine-year-olds and under ed. Kit Wright, illus. Michael Foreman (Viking Kestrel/Puffin paperback)
This is a wide-ranging collection, including the work of established poets as well as that of modern writers

such as Michael Rosen, Roger McGough, Robert Frost and the editor himself. The illustrations are agreeable, but not obtrusive, the whole an excellent book for dipping into. Heartily recommended for home, as well as school use.

*The Queen Elizabeth Story Rosemary Sutcliff,
illus. C. Walter Hodges (Oxford)

Rainboat Lace Kendall, illus. Charles Keeping
(Hamish Hamilton)
This is an outstanding book for upper-level eight-year-olds. A boy in eighteenth-century Florida is made homeless by a flood. He is rescued by Shem, a huge black man who has been a slave, as are Amity and Jonas, two other children, and numerous animals. Charles Keeping's illustrations are brilliant, but it is the text itself that stays in the mind. The characters come alive; Shem himself, a Noah-like figure, is truly memorable.

*The Shrinking of Treehorn Florence Parry Heide,
illus. Edward Gorey (Viking Kestrel/Puffin paperback)

*Stig of the Dump Clive King, illus. Edward Ardizzone
(Viking Kestrel/Puffin paperback)

Stories for Christmas Alison Uttley, chosen by Kathleen
Lines, illus. Gavin Rowe (Faber/Puffin paperback)
Twelve superb stories by a classic storyteller, chosen by an editor of discrimination. Alison Uttley was brought up in the country towards the end of the last century, before the true commercialization of Christmas had begun. Her stories reflect a quality of magic and security which will enhance every modern child's experience. The illustrations are pleasant and appropriate, but the tales stand alone.

*_Swallowdale_ and *_Swallows and Amazons_ Arthur Ransome
(Cape/Puffin paperback)

Toby's Millions Morris Lurie, illus. Arthur Horner
(Puffin paperback)
> Toby, digging a deep, deep hole in the back yard, finds
> not one, but three chests of treasure. They prove to be
> worth twenty-three million pounds, and change his
> family's life in ways which could not have been
> foreseen. The story is fast-moving and funny, but
> thought-provoking, too. The black-and-white
> illustrations are lively, and liberally sprinkled. A sure
> success, read aloud at home or school.

*_Tom's Midnight Garden_ Philippa Pearce,
illus. Susan Einzig (Oxford/Puffin paperback)

Tottie: The Story of a Dolls' House Rumer Godden,
illus. Joanna Jamieson (Puffin paperback)
> Originally published as _The Dolls' House_ in 1947, this is
> a superb book. Rumer Godden breathes life into a
> family of dolls without depriving them of their essential
> doll nature. Tottie Plantagenet is a farthing doll more
> than a century old; along with Mr Plantagenet, his
> wife Birdie and a tiny plush boy doll called Apple (and
> a pipe-cleaner dog called Darner) she lives in an
> antique dolls' house which was inherited by two little
> girls, Emily and Charlotte. Then the evil, beautiful
> kid-and-china doll Marchpane, known to Tottie in her
> earlier days, arrives to join the group. A memorable
> book, in which there is tragedy, as well as triumph, as
> the tale is worked out.

*_The Wool-Pack_ Cynthia Harnett (Methuen/Puffin
paperback)

CLASSICS

Alice in Wonderland and *Through the Looking Glass* Lewis
Carroll, illus. John Tenniel 2 volumes in slipcase
(Macmillan)
This is surely the most satisfying form in which to own
the two Alice titles. Each volume is well-proportioned
and sturdy, with remarkably large, clear text, the
original black-and-white illustrations and, as well, the
colour plates prepared by the artist himself for the
1911 edition. A wonderful gift for an Alice lover; or
any child. (*Alice* is also available in a range of editions,
including a Puffin paperback.)

Black Beauty Anna Sewell (Dent Illustrated Classics/
Puffin paperback)

The Jungle Book Rudyard Kipling (Macmillan/
Macmillan paperback)

Just So Stories Rudyard Kipling (Macmillan, Quarto
Edition/Macmillan paperback)
This is a magnificent book, beautifully produced and
equally well proportioned. Its extra-large print
commends it to young readers (as well as grandparents
with failing eyesight!) and its author's own original line
drawings are detailed and fascinating.

King Arthur and his Knights Anthony Mockler,
illus. Nick Harris (Oxford)
This is an outstanding book; beautifully designed and
produced, with clear text, splendid black-and-white
illustrations at every chapter head, and twelve colour
plates. Only the most literary eight-year-olds are ready
for Arthur, but this edition is so approachable that
many such children will love it. The style is spirited,
and reads aloud well.

*One Thousand and One Arabian Nights Geraldine McCaugh-
rean, illus. Stephen Lavis (Oxford University Press)

*Robin Hood Bernard Miles, illus. Victor Ambrus
(Hamlyn)
Complete with map, and background information
which contrives to enthral rather than bore, this is a
startlingly good version of the Robin Hood legend. The
illustrations have dramatic impact and will be
examined again and again. The tales are told with
verve and clarity; the whole, large format volume is a
delight to handle, read and, if possible, own. (For
upper level listeners and readers mainly. This is
probably a ten-plus book, but its visual appeal will
endear it to able eights.)

*Treasure Island Robert Louis Stevenson (Dent
Illustrated Classics/Puffin paperback)

*The Wind in the Willows Kenneth Grahame,
illus. Ernest Shepard (Methuen/Methuen paperback)

The Wizard of Oz L. Frank Baum, illus. Michael Hague
(Methuen)
First published in 1900 as The Wonderful Wizard of Oz
and illustrated by many different artists over the
intervening years, this recommended edition has large
print and copious, distinctive pictures in Michael
Hague's favourite earthy tones. The story is a spirited
one: Dorothy, a child of the Kansas plains, is carried
off by a cyclone and joins the Scarecrow, the Tin
Woodman and the Cowardly Lion in their search for
Oz, the great wizard, who can give them each their
dearest wish. (Dorothy's is, understandably, to be
returned home!) The uncomplicated nature of the
action—fast-moving and cheerful most of the time—
makes the book a good 'early classic'. The illustrations
make this edition a book to treasure.

6

Learning to Read

It is natural to believe that there must be a simple way of teaching children to read: a one-plus-one-equals-two method which needs only to be applied at the right time to achieve the desired results.

Since written English uses a total of twenty-six letters (our alphabet), it is just as natural to believe that this ideal method will rely on teaching children to recognize these letters. Assembling them into words is the next step, and assembling these words into sentences is the final step. Task accomplished.

But is it? In my work, I am constantly confronted by nine- and ten-year-old children who certainly know their alphabet, and can recognize letters. Most of them also have a grasp of 'phonics', that system of 'sounding out' by which many people believe reading can be mastered. But they cannot read, except in the most stumbling, word-by-word manner. Why? What has gone wrong in their schooling, or their homes—or in society as a whole—to prevent these children from becoming fluent readers?

A little reflection on the nature of reading is probably advisable at this point. It is worth noting also that, regardless of the teaching methods in favour at any particular time, the nature of the learning task does not change. If we think of reading as a process by which meaning is transferred from the mind of a writer to the mind of a reader, using the medium of print on a page, we can see that the seventeenth-century child, poring over the Bible, was facing the same challenge as the modern child, gazing at a brightly illustrated picture book. (This earlier child may even have had an advantage; only children of a privileged social class learned to read in the seventeenth century, and these children were accustomed to hearing the Bible read aloud, morning and evening.)

Even the most informed scientists still have little idea as to how the brain processes print to effect this transfer of meaning. It is easy to see how this fact limits the 'teaching' of reading! I would go so far as to claim that we cannot, with confidence, 'teach' reading; we must confine our efforts to helping children *learn* to read.

Sometimes a child seems to have made little progress in reading after a year or so at school. Parents may become alarmed; could there be something the matter with the child? (They may have heard of certain conditions, such as dyslexia . . .)

There is certainly a rare child who, though of average or above average intelligence, experiences extreme difficulty in learning to read. But 'rare' is the word to note here. Experts believe that only one child in many thousands has a 'specific learning disability' as they prefer to call such a condition. ('Dyslexia' means simply 'unable to read'. Most specialists avoid the term.)

There is no special part of the brain which houses reading ability. How could there be? Reading is not an in-born capacity, like walking. It has been developed by human beings, along with writing, as an extra way of communicating, person to person. Of course, severe damage to the brain may make it impossible for a person to learn to read, but such damage is likely to cause learning difficulties in all areas, not merely in reading. One is fairly safe in assuming that a child who has learned to talk is also equipped for the reading task.

From time to time we hear startling news about reading, from the media. 'Children taught to read by computer' ran a headline recently. One can envisage ways in which electronic devices might help some children in the early stages of reading acquisition, certainly, but we need not be over-impressed. Learning must still, as ever, take place in the mind of the learner. Replacing teacher or parent as agent between child and book has its pitfalls. Evidence abounds that personal, human contact and communication is vital to the learning process, especially in the early stages, and, surely, we are inviting trouble if we banish *the book* from early reading experience?

In trying to understand what a child must do to learn to read, it may be useful to consider the child who learns to read alone, or to use a common phrase, 'teaches herself to read'. This child does what must be done to learn, without apparent help or instruction; but, most importantly, she understands the nature of the task—she knows that reading means 'getting the message'. This established, the determined child (and this child must be determined) brings everything she can conjure from her verbal and visual repertoire to help with the task: imagination, recalled vocabulary, innate knowledge of the way language fits together to make sense. She realizes very early on that one is not truly reading until one's eyes are swinging along the line while the meaning pours into the mind, and she practises this skill. She asks questions of anyone at hand, and draws conclusions.

In short, this child accepts the printed page as a source of meaning, and sets about finding a way of extracting this meaning; of discovering how written language operates to convey sense to the reader. She realizes that letters, alone and in combination, *must* be pointers to meaning, but that other clues are available too, and, indeed, must be used in pursuit of meaning. Consequently, she will experiment with emphasis and rhythm, and use clues of context almost automatically.

Children who are vigorously grappling with the reading task in this way will read the following sentences with assurance, unconsciously accepting that, in each, the word 'row' is pronounced differently and has a different meaning, though the spelling is identical.

'I will *row* the boat.'
'I heard a big *row*.'

These children are learning what must be done to read. Their way of handling print is flexible, rather than rigid. They are venturing boldly, rather than following slavishly. They are on the way to success.

Naturally, some children will be better than others at this 'making sense of printed language'—just as certain children, in any group, will be better at learning gymnastics, or mastering musical skills, than others. We may speculate about the relative merits of natural ability and enthusiasm (or motivation, as teachers call it), but no reliable conclusion is possible. It is easy to see, however, how each factor quickens and bolsters the other.

The child who is determined to learn, in any field, usually attends to the task in hand with senses alert, and quickly masters a few elementary skills. By the same token, the child with 'natural' ability may experience some early success very easily, and become enthused as a result. Both of these children will probably move smoothly on to a learning programme which is self-reinforcing. The better they become, the more they practise, with increasingly effective results.

Obviously, as parents, our task is to help our children join the ranks of these successful learners; a job for which we are well equipped, if we give some thought to the nature of the task, and use our resources wisely.

OLD, NEW—AND ETERNAL—METHODS

It is understandable that the parents of children who are about to start school should be interested in 'methods'. 'How will my child be taught to read?' is uppermost in many minds. Doubt and suspicion seem to surround so-called 'new' methods. Can we be sure that schools these days are doing their jobs efficiently? Didn't the old-fashioned 'phonics' method work for us, and for even earlier generations? Isn't it a help to know that you can 'work words out', c-a-t spells cat, to use a hackneyed example? (Pity the poor cats of the world! It is a great wonder that our youthful ancestors did not drown the lot of them!)

Older people are inclined to claim that they 'learned to read by phonics', when, actually, they have no way of knowing *how* they learned to read; only that they did, and that their teachers introduced them to certain facts about written language which seemed to be essential to the process. This is sensible enough. It would be nonsense to suggest that the English alphabet had nothing to do with reading. Unfortunately, most of us cannot remember—or do not recognize as significant—the other factors and experiences in our early lives which helped us to learn to read: our own use and understanding of spoken language, the examples of adults around us in both reading themselves and reading or telling stories to us, the signs and notices which surrounded us, and our own expectation of being able to read better and better, as we grew older. Many of us who were at school fifty years ago have forgotten that we were given a book on our first day and encouraged (expected, actually) to launch ourselves upon it. Do we really believe that our teachers intended us to use *only* phonics? And if so, why were the stories so wonderfully, so helpfully repetitive?

> 'Run, run as fast as you can,
> You can't catch me, I'm the Gingerbread Man!'

and

> 'Who will help me plant the wheat?' asked the Little
> Red Hen.
> 'Not I,' said the cat.
> 'Not I,' said the dog.
> 'Not I,' said the mouse.
> 'Then I will plant it myself,' said the Little Red Hen.
> And she did.

Heady stuff, to the 'new entrant'! (A modern phrase; in my day, if you were there, you were *there*.)

I am certain that our teachers expected us to learn these stories by heart, and knew that this rote repetition would help us to learn to read. Tying up what one sees on the page with what one knows in one's head is a mighty step in the right direction. And experiencing early success is vital. Anyone working with young children knows that!

Of course phonics helped a little if one faltered, but this has never been doubted in any age, and is certainly recognized today. Just as certainly, however, we know that an over-concentration on phonics in early reading is unlikely to produce early mastery, and that it can inhibit the acquisition of other, more potentialy useful skills.

The best teachers in any age have used their own feeling for, and knowledge of, children, language and books, to bring these three together in joyful communion, and to make sure that the mixture jelled. No age or culture has had the monopoly of this sort of teaching. I experienced it when I first entered school at the hands of an elderly teacher who would be one hundred and twenty, if she were alive today. She was strict, in the way of her generation, and she cared deeply about us, and about books. She read aloud to us every single day, and one might have heard a pin drop. I was enchanted, snared, and have been held captive ever since in the web she cast around books, and the children in her care.

But the phonics theory is a persuasive one. I cannot expect the non-specialist reader to accept its limitations without both describing it, and explaining my own misgivings about its use in isolation. Hence the following section.

PHONICS, AS A METHOD
WHAT IT IS, HOW IT HELPS, AND HOW IT HINDERS

If we examine any page of text, we will search in vain for more than twenty-six different letters. These constitute the English alphabet, and are the letters we must all use for writing. 'And recognize for reading,' you may say. If that were all there were to reading, all would be simple.

Learning to recognize twenty-six letters, even in their large and small forms, is a relatively simple task. However, whether we like it or not, there are approximately forty *sounds* in English, as against these twenty-six *letters*. 'But', you may say, 'aren't the extra sounds produced by combining letters? Ch, ph, gh, oo, ou, ea, for example?' Yes, but here too, complications abound, for no single combination has only one sound. (Using only the examples given above, think of *ch*ild and *ch*orus, ele*ph*ant and she*ph*erd, *gh*ost and thou*gh*, b*oo*k and bl*oo*d, thr*ou*gh and c*ou*gh, r*ea*dy and br*ea*the.)

The fact is that we must teach our children to read using twenty-six letters, not one of which represents one sound only, and all of which have constantly irregular pronunciations in their various combinations, all depending on historical development, not on the logic we would like to think prevails. But logic does prevail, you may say, with ran, fan, man, ban, can, van, pan, tan. Yes, but what about cough, rough, bough, though, through and enough?

It has often been suggested that we should 'reform' the written language, providing, once and for all, one letter for one sound. The trouble with this suggestion is that every dialect would then need its own alphabet. No American child could be expected to recognize 'far' any longer in any British book, where it would be encoded as 'fah' instead of the 'farr' form dictated by American usage. How many separate alphabets would be needed for the British Isles alone? The mind reels.

No, written language is tied to *meaning*, not sound. It is meant to be *read*. Naturally, when reading aloud, we all use the accent or dialect which comes most naturally to us, in terms of our upbringing and education. Keeping the spelling reasonably constant allows each of us, wherever we come from in the English-speaking world, to read what another person from any other part has written, despite these differences.

Still, faith in 'sounding out' may persist. The method sounds so reasonable, and it does provide teachers and parents with something positive to *do*. At the very least, some people reason, starting with phonics is sensible. After all, the words used in the earliest stages of reading are all simple. Why not use phonics at this stage, even if we must move on to other methods later? Unfortunately, this attractive and plausible argument has immediate pitfalls.

As it happens, the most common words—those which young children use in their speech every day—seem to flout the phonic laws in a way which can only be described as outrageous! Think of the word 'a' as in 'a house'. You have already taught the child that the *letter* 'a' says 'a' as in 'hat'. But here, in this important little word, it says 'u' as in 'hut'. Move on to 'was', another essential little word. Unfortunately, the 'a' in 'was' is pronounced 'o' as in 'hot'.

Faced with these contradictions, and having espoused the phonic cause, you are obliged to choose two courses of action: you can say nothing and hope that the child does not notice that your theory has fallen down, or you can explain that 'a' and 'was' are both exceptions, and must be learned. In the first instance, you will be guilty of evasion (if not deception). In the second, you will be introducing a concept which you will then have to explain. (Five-year-olds are not strong on 'exceptions'.)

But let us get on. For this 'simple' teaching project you will certainly need the words mother, whole, water, over, through, their, love, many, could, friend, want—all ordinary enough words, surely? The thing they have in common, unfortunately, is that they cannot be read correctly using phonics.

Of course, you can cheat and confine your children to specially written texts which *do* obey the rules. Then you fetch up with passages like this:

> Get Tom's dog his meat.
> Eat the meat, Dan.

Dan eats the meat.
'Good dog, Dan,' says Tom.

However, you must not deceive the child into believing that the 'ea' in 'eat' and 'meat' will remain constant (think of 'ready' and 'great'), or that the 'oo' sound in 'good' is any more reliable (what of 'root' and 'blood'?), but perhaps you may safely ignore these anomalies and still press on with the phonic system. After all, thousands—even millions—of children have learned to read this way in the past, haven't they? My suspicion is that most children discover fairly quickly what must be done in order to learn to read, and do it. Naturally, most of this learning is unconscious, as in so many other fields. Is any child of average intelligence likely to go on believing that the application of phonic skills alone will enable her to become a fluent reader, when evidence abounds that most words are exceptions, and must be read using other clues, cues and resources?

My further suspicion is that the phonic tradition continues because it is the only system available which seems to provide teachers and parents with a course of positive action. In short, it *seems* to be a one-and-one-make-two method, as against 'airy-fairy' approaches based on 'experience' (always to be regarded with suspicion!). Most of us still harbour a puritanical streak; children should have to wrestle with symbols in a real 'work' situation! (Years ago our youngest child's school entry was deferred for a year through a health problem. When she entered school at six, she was reading fluently, though no effort had been made to 'teach' her. Even the teacher of her class gave off a strong feeling of disapproval; it just wasn't *fair* that this child should have done better than those children who had been coming earnestly to school, rain or shine . . .)

You are now justified in asking:

IF NOT PHONICS AS A STARTING-POINT, THEN WHAT?

For the moment, a word of reassurance, and a few suggestions. Children are equipped for learning to read by the sheer possession of their miraculously functioning brains, their immense store of experience and their previous and wonderful accomplishments in the language-learning field. No computer yet invented (or likely to be) has the potential for creative thought and action which is contained in the mind and body of a five-year-old child. There should be no room for anxiety in *our* minds—only confidence, and pleasure in the existence of this unique, superbly equipped individual, along with a conviction that our help, support and encouragement will be a major strength in every field of his or her life. And we *can* help!

In learning to read, knowing about books and how they work to convey information and to tell stories is the absolute, fundamental and first step. We must not assume that children will automatically understand the nature of the task—what reading *is*. This must be demonstrated, and is best accomplished through shared contact with real books. A child watching an adult mend a chair, bake a cake, or mow a lawn, can see what is happening and even copy some of the actions. Not so the child watching an adult immersed in a book—unless that adult is prepared to act as go-between, and share the book with the child.

The well-prepared child of five has spent many hundreds of hours, from earliest days, listening to stories, handling books, asking questions and responding to answers. Little wonder that this child is ready for a flying start at school. If you feel that your child may not be quite so well prepared, it is never too late to begin making up for lost time. Use the suggestions given in Chapter 1, and prepare for fun yourself. For children's books *are* fun.

Try to fit in read-aloud sessions at any time, at least twice daily, if possible. If need be, practise your read-aloud skills ahead of time—you will want to read the story before you present it to the youngster, anyway, to avoid launching into something which gives *you* little pleasure. (Parents have rights, too.) Then, start exploring books with your child—

not worrying about individual words, but drawing the youngster's attention to the way books *work* to provide meaning. Covers and title pages can be looked at closely; many of them are beautifully designed, and some books still have lovely, decorated endpapers glued to the inside of both front and back covers, and carried on to the opposite page.

Show the child what is written on the *spine*, using the correct term and pointing to title and author as you read, '*Flat Stanley* by Jeff Brown'. Many children are fascinated to discover that the tiny print on the back of the title page will even tell you where the book was *printed* and *bound*—all new ideas which help to make the book itself a known, less mysterious object.

Make sure, in a casual way, that the child knows that the human voice takes its cue from the printed text, not from the picture. This can be done without any air of 'teaching' (which might well frighten the youngster away), by pointing to the start of the first line of text and saying, 'Look, here's where the story begins', and promptly starting. Run your finger smoothly along beneath the words for several lines, and then give up.

The child will quickly get the idea that the reader knows what to say by following the black squiggles, that they always say the same thing in the same book, and that one's eyes start on the lefthand side of the top line, travel along to the end and then return *to the left again.* (In real life, and if lines were paths, sensible people would return on the second line from right to left!) And can we be sure that the school-starter knows where the *left* is, what a *line* is, or even how to identify the first page? What about the concept of a 'word'?—or the notion that a group of squiggles 'says' something? ('Saying' surely means speaking; nothing can be heard from those mysterious black marks!) The way books work to provide us with meaning can be either a total mystery or, literally, 'an open book' to young children.

The best way to identify stories which suit your individual style is to try out a wide range. When reading stories from a collection, it is useful to keep a notebook on hand, and jot down relevant details: date read, title and author of story, title and compiler of anthology, page number, and both your own and the children's reactions. Make notes to improve future presentations ('Pause before last paragraph to increase impact.' 'Leave time for laughter after separate incidents.') Aim at a steady improvement in your technique. A red sticker against a title on your list to mark your own most successful stories allows for easy identification, especially if you note the source of the actual book. The best teachers—and all sensible parents—build up a wide selection of their own favourite anthologies over the years. Nothing is more infuriating than finding that the book you want at this very moment is *not* in the library. To discover that it has been lost and is irreplaceable because out of print can be a tragedy!

For obvious reasons, write your name firmly in the front of all your books. A valid part of book use is lending and borrowing; but only if all parties respect the rights of original owners.

As light relief, I must share with you a story told me by a teacher in Australia last year. Noting that her three-year-old grandson's eyes always went immediately to the illustration when she turned a page while reading to him, she endeavoured to draw his attention to the text. 'Oh,' he said airily, 'I don't need to look at that. That's just for people who can't read the pictures!'

Becoming aware of the twenty-six letters of the alphabet is essential, and fortunately not difficult. Almost all children know their 'own' letter, or initial, and are eager, once they start, to master those of other family members. Our world is full of print; almost everything we eat, wear, play with and work with is labelled, and signs, directions and notices abound. Once children start noticing letters and words there is usually no stopping them; but they sometimes need our help in starting. ('See where it says "Post Office" up there? That's where we will post our letter.') 'I Spy' and other similar games help with the learning of initial letters—which is probably the most useful skill of all, in the phonic range. (Some would say the *only* useful aspect of phonics in the early days.) Alphabet books and wall friezes come in a vast variety of colours and styles, and will certainly help, too.

Once the child is giving some attention to print, regular features will be noticed, and may be reinforced. 'I', 'a' and 'the' occur so often that they virtually need no teaching—and the repetitive books that your child is given at school soon ensure that other words are learned in context, with no difficulty.

FROM THE MIND TO THE PAGE: THE STRUCTURE OF LANGUAGE

An enormous, but often unrecognized strength of beginning readers, if they are not restricted to a word-by-word method, is their unconscious knowledge of the way their own language is constructed. In such a sentence as, ' "Now we have no more cookies to eat," said Toad sadly,' almost every word could be only that part of speech which it is. The six-year-old reading this sentence is unlikely to have heard of nouns, verbs and adverbs, but she will *sense* that 'have' (after 'we') is a verb, that 'cookies' is a noun, and that 'sadly' is certainly an adverb. Think how this instinctive knowledge of the structure of one's own language narrows the field! The child's task in reading this sentence does not compare in difficulty with the problem posed by identifying single words out of context—a fact which is often overlooked by those who see reading as individual word-solving. In 'real' reading, as against word-solving, any particular word can be only one of several alternatives, if it is to make sense. Giving our children the expectation of *sense* from their reading is clearly all-important. Remember, too, that children cannot be expected to make sense of constructions which do not occur in their own speech, or listening experiences. Consider such a sentence as:

'Wise Owl, their father, who was much much older than all of them, had so many feathers that they went all round his head like a crown, and trailed in a double row down his back.'

This might be classed as seven-year-old material, and comes from a book which most seven- and eight-year-olds enjoy. (*Little Bear's Feather* by Evelyn Davies, Hamish Hamilton.) But the child reading it cannot be expected to read the above sentence, unless she knows that the clause beginning with 'who . . .' is to be held in the mind as describing 'Wise Owl, their father', until the verb 'had' is finally encountered. She may even imagine that 'had' applies to 'all of them', which, after all, comes just before it; in which case she has little hope of making sense of the sentence. The ability to solve each word, while undeniably useful, will not produce unqualified success if you accept that reading means 'getting the meaning'. What children need are 'the patterns of language' for reference, in their minds.

Fortunately, as a parent, you need not worry too much about these intricacies. The way to avoid or reduce such confusions is to make sure that children *do* have the structures of language securely laid down in their minds, so that what is seen on the page ties up with remembered and familiar patterns. And the source of these patterns lies in 'book language'.

Book language is different from everyday, spoken language. Even the simplest stories observe certain formal conventions with which children must be familiar, if they are to read fluently. Children who are familiar with these conventions have an enormous advantage. The child whose background has not prepared him for sudden confrontation with the mysteries of written language needs gentle handling and a wealth of supporting experience: *book* experience.

READING: TO HEAR OR NOT TO HEAR?

You are likely to be wondering by now what I am going to

say about 'hearing' children's reading. My advice is simple: 'Don't, unless the child *wants* to read to you, in order to demonstrate his or her skill.'

Hearing a child read aloud is a 'test' situation; of use to the specialist as a way of assessing accomplishment, and diagnosing difficulty, but little more. Either a child *can* read a passage we decide to 'hear', in which case the performance has no value, or he can't. In the latter case, we are allowing him to experience failure, and simultaneously striking a blow for the belief that reading is a difficult and unpleasant affair. Many children are acutely embarrassed by their own imagined limitations when asked to perform in this way. The whole thought of books and reading may become a night-mare to them—a tragic situation which in itself contributes to failure. For enjoyment is a necessary condition of learning, in any area, in the early stages.

Because I don't believe that any amount of advice will prevent people from using time-honoured procedures (and putting children through this particular torture is certainly an established feature of our culture), I give my Reading Centre parents a practical alternative: reading *with* children. This is a shared experience, to which child and adult both contribute.

It goes like this. Decide on a book which is fairly simple but has a bit of spirit (like *Mrs Gaddy and the Ghost* by Wilson Gage) and settle yourself comfortably with the child. Inspect cover, title page and any other interesting feature, and then turn to the first page. Say to the child, 'Let's try reading it aloud together,' and begin at once, moving your finger smoothly along the line as you speak. If the child does not start immediately, don't worry; the procedure is compulsive once started. In all likelihood, she will join in, her voice fractionally behind yours.

To begin with, *you* will be doing all the reading; but gradually, you will develop a feeling for the points at which the child can take over for a few words, or lines. And of course you can give *any* book this treatment, depending on the age and reading level of the child concerned: from the simplest pre-reader to an interesting novel. An inspired teacher I know persuaded her school principal to sanction the purchase of multiple copies of a number of exciting, well-written novels for the eleven- and twelve-year-olds she was teaching. Then she spent one half-hour twice daily reading her copy aloud, while each child followed the story silently in his or her own copy. The standard of reading in this class rose steeply. Just as importantly, the children's interest in reading novels during their own time increased markedly. The school library was besieged!

In both the situations described (parent reading with child at home and teacher reading to children at school) the key factor is the provision of *support* for the child; the adult supplies the phrasing, or patterning, giving the child the chance to take part in a real reading experience.

This is, of course, what the 'naturally' good reader does for herself: propels her eye along a line of print with the intention of getting the meaning. Clues are picked up from a variety of sources—illustrations, the title of the story, a few familiar words and more than a few inspired guesses. Increasingly, phonics *will* help; for example, to give the first clue as to what a word must be. (If a man is riding an animal, it could be a horse, a donkey or a mule; if it begins with 'd' the choice is clear.) Knowledge of the plural 's', which is reasonably regular, and of the ending '-ing' which is (blessedly!) always the same, will certainly help; but the greatest strength of all will be the help which the child is given, through your support, in swinging his eyes along the line while the meaning passes into his mind. This will set the scene for his own performance, and give him the confidence to try.

A warning is justified at this point. If you are over-anxious about your child's progress, your tension may be conveyed to the child during book sessions which have a teaching flavour. This will certainly do more harm than good, and may prevent the very progress you are trying to achieve.

Unless you feel quite relaxed about the whole subject, it is better to spend all available 'book' time reading aloud to the child, from books which will interest and delight him. (Never from 'graded readers'.) This is not only certain to help in a proven and positive way, but will keep your relationship with your child in good order. And this is the most important consideration of all.

Let me finish this section with a reassuring quotation from the work of Professor Frank Smith, an international authority on the subject of reading.

'In the first ten years of their lives, children develop a spoken language vocabulary that enables them to recognize and make sense of at least 20,000 words, nearly eight words a day. And at the same time children are also acquiring the knowledge that enables them to identify on sight hundreds of faces and many thousands of objects; to recall ages, birthdays, telephone numbers, addresses and prices; to sing songs and master the rules of games; to find their way around buildings, streets and fields. The number of different objects we learn to distinguish and recognize is literally uncountable. Among such a multitude, the memorization of written words, with all the meaning that can be brought to them, is a rippling stream that loses significance as it becomes part of a broad river.'

Can we doubt, in the face of this, that our children are equipped for the task—the rewarding, exhilarating task—of learning to read?

For an excellent, easy-to-read and very thorough account of this subject, read Margaret Meek's book, *Learning to Read*, published by The Bodley Head.

To Conclude . . .

'The gift of fantasy has meant more to me than my gift for absorbing positive knowledge.'

Einstein, late in life.

I believe that the years from five to eight are crucial ones for producing readers, and that producing readers is a critical undertaking for the human race. Books are rooted in language, and language is the raw material of thought. If we want our children to do their own thinking, we must ensure that they learn to use language precisely, sensitively, flexibly. This means that they must read.

One might describe the years between five and nine as years of apprenticeship to reading. It is certainly true that the earliest period of all—from birth to perhaps five—can be said to lay the foundations for all future learning. Just as certainly, however, this second period must be a time of bridge-building, if the desirable opposite shore—that point by which children have become truly capable and autonomous learners and livers—is to be reached.

Machines are all very well for helping to relieve us of some of the more tedious of our daily tasks, for relaxation and for providing facts, fast. But for thinking and feeling? We are each of us equipped with an inbuilt, personal thinking and feeling machine which makes the most sophisticated modern computer look like a medieval contraption. Our human-ness gives us the capacity to look at ourselves, at each other and at the world, to reflect and to grow in wisdom.

We must be alert to the fact that this priceless capacity, the essential and unique property of humankind, is in danger of erosion. We must cling to our right to think, to wonder, to arrive at decisions and take action. We must make sure that our children are not only equipped for these tasks, but convinced of their value. I believe that we can do this, and that helping children to become committed and responsive readers constitutes a huge step in the right direction.

Don't let anyone tell you that reading is a mere hobby, or that the world is moving on from paper and print. The wisdom of the ages resides in books, and the things our children need to face life *now*. 'Where is the wisdom we have lost in knowledge?' asked T. S. Eliot. 'Where is the knowledge we have lost in information?'

There *is* no substitute for wisdom, and the world needs wisdom now as never before. Let us do our own thinking, and see to it that our children grow up doing theirs. That way lies satisfaction with a chance of survival.

Index

Index

Index